Wading the World Wide Web

Wading the World Wide Web

Internet Activities for Beginners

Keith Kyker

1998
Libraries Unlimited, Inc.
and Its Division
Teacher Ideas Press
Englewood, Colorado

Dedication

This book is dedicated to everyone who believes that children and learning are more important than hardware and software. You know who you are. Remember: love kids, teach school, and keep the faith.

Diagrams by Lincoln Logos
Illustrations by Mike Lalone

LIBRARIES UNLIMITED, INC.
and Its Division
Teacher Ideas Press
P.O. Box 6633
Englewood, CO 80155-6633
(800) 237-6124
www.lu.com/tip

Constance Hardesty, *Project Editor*
Sheryl Tongue, *Design and Composition*
Susan Konarske, *Proofreader*

Library of Congress Cataloging-in-Publication Data

Kyker, Keith.
Wading the World Wide Web : Internet activities for beginners / Keith Kyker.
xvii, 170 p. 22×28 cm.
Includes index.
ISBN 1-56308-605-0
1. Internet (Computer network) 2. World Wide Web (Information retrieval system) I. Title.
TK5105.875.I57K95 1998
004.67'8--dc21 98-18615
CIP

Contents

Figures

Preface

It is spring, 1998. I'm a middle-school media specialist by trade, and so far it's been a busy year. I'm catching up on some small writing assignments (columns, reviews, and articles) and my most recent book is at the publisher. I hope to take a short vacation soon. And I'm thinking about some special activities for the school year.

I've used the World Wide Web to help me with many of these tasks. Here's a list of a few Web sites that I've visited:

- **The Alabama State Parks Home Page**—My ideal vacation is renting a rustic cabin in a state or national park, away from phones, faxes, and the Internet, and traipsing around in the woods for a few days. If I can get some canoeing in, that's all the better. I used this site to select a park for my mini-vacation.
- **The FAME Home Page**—FAME is the Florida Association of Media Educators. I've just learned that I'll be speaking at its conference this fall, so I went to its Web site to get some information.
- **The Alabama Shakespeare Festival Home Page**—Did you know that Alabama has one of the world's best Shakespeare festivals? It's true. I'm checking to see which plays they've selected for this season. Maybe this year I'll take a few eighth-graders on a field trip to see a real Shakespearean play.
- **ESPN Sportszone**—I'm a basketball fan. My favorite team is the Orlando Magic. On this page, I learned that the Magic just re-signed one of my favorite players to a long-term contract. (Boy, I wish teachers got paid that much!)
- **Panasonic Broadcast and Digital Systems**—A friend is the media specialist at a new school in my district. I told her that I'd help her order the school TV production equipment, and this site gave me some updates on the Panasonic product line.
- **Yamaha Music Infostation**—My daughter wants to learn how to play electronic keyboards. I saw an advertisement for a Yamaha keyboard, but the store is about 50 miles away. The Yamaha site

gave me a full description of the keyboard and a suggested price. Looks like a good buy.

- **The Weather Channel**—I'd like to go to the beach this weekend, so I took a peek at the regional Doppler radar.
- **The Florida Statutes**—I spend a week each summer at a central Florida beach community. This is a favorite site for nesting sea turtles, and I know there's a law saying people are supposed to keep their distance as these gentle giants make their way up the shoreline to dig their nests. Still, every year, some ill-mannered tourist is on the beach with a flashlight, harassing the mama sea turtles. I'm writing a letter to the community's local newspaper. This Web site lets me quote the law with confidence, as I encourage local hotel managers to advise their guests about this law.
- **The Libraries Unlimited Home Page**—I don't know—maybe it's just a sense of loyalty, but I check this page whenever I'm on the Web. It is a great site to learn about some fantastic books.

Why do I share this list with you? Am I recommending these sites for everyone? Of course not! These are a few of the sites *I* use. Depending on where you live and your hobbies and interests, these pages may be great additions to your bookmark file—or they may have no value at all.

The Internet is a tool. The Internet is a big book. The Internet saves me time and money and makes me more informed. But I'm not finished with some of my tasks.

- I should call the park rangers at the park I've selected. I bet they can recommend a cabin near the river and the hiking trails.
- I should write a letter to the Alabama Shakespeare Festival Office. Maybe someone will tell me about special educational discounts, or a chance for my students to meet some of the actors.
- A visit to my local Panasonic vendor will help me build a valuable business contact in the community. (And if the equipment breaks, I can't e-mail it to the Web site for repair.)
- I really should call my state legislator to let him know how I feel about the endangered sea turtles. Most laws begin with a single phone call, letter, or office visit.

What's my point? The Internet can be a good beginning, and even a decent middle, but it is rarely an adequate end. The World Wide Web is a great resource, but don't let it substitute for real life. It's like the difference between shooting a bullet and throwing it.

This is the message we must impart to our students. The Internet is full of data that can enrich our lives, but we can't confuse data with knowledge, learning, and understanding.

Thanks to the World Wide Web, an immeasurable amount of data is now available in libraries and classrooms. Learning to access, process, and synthesize this data is an important information skill for our students. I hope I have created a book that will help you teach your students how to use this resource.

Just make sure to take them out for recess when you're finished.

Wading the Web Site

The book you're holding, *Wading the World Wide Web,* is supported by its very own Web site. Here's the address:

http://www.schooltv.com/wading.htm

On this Web site, you'll find a page of hyperlinks that take you directly to the Web sites used in this book. You'll also find helpful suggestions on how to integrate the World Wide Web into the curriculum, additional technology links, and the opportunity to e-mail the author. I'd love to hear your comments and suggestions as you use this book in your school. Why not recommend a Web site for the next edition of *Wading the World Wide Web*?

As you know, the World Wide Web is an ever-changing medium. In the future, I will do my best to provide replacements for activities whose Web sites disappear from the Web. This will be a great way for you to maintain a working collection of *Wading* exercises until the next edition of this book is published.

So take off your shoes, log on to the Web, and begin *Wading*.

Introduction

I am a middle-school media specialist. In the spring of 1996, I was informed that our school would soon get complete Internet access. As a media educator, I was quite competent with a personal computer and I had kept up-to-date on the lore and lingo of the Internet. I'd even subscribed to America Online *before* AOL offered Internet access, but dropped it because I didn't feel the proprietary information it offered justified the expense. In other words, I knew about computers and communication, but I really wasn't experienced on the World Wide Web.

For a couple of years, I'd heard about the World Wide Web and all the "cool" Web sites and chat rooms, but honestly, I had no real interest in awakening this sleeping giant. But my school was getting all this technology, and I was determined to educate myself. A few days earlier, I had received a mail ad from an Internet provider (not America Online, CompuServe, or any other major commercial provider), so I gave them a call and signed up for their Internet service at a flat rate of $20 per month. Soon I was exploring the World Wide Web.

That was the easy part.

The hard part was finding something worthwhile to investigate. Like every consumer, I'd been bombarded with uniform resource locators (URLs—you know, the things that start with **http://www ...**) from TV commercials and magazine advertisements, so I typed them in. Most of those Web sites were just glorified commercials. Then a colleague told me about search engines and bookmarks. I began searching the World Wide Web and bookmarking interesting Web sites that I found. A trip to the bookstore garnered Web site directories in book form and magazines that reviewed Web sites. At a media convention, I purchased *The Internet Resource Directory for K–12 Teachers and Librarians* (Libraries Unlimited, annual), which has been an excellent resource for worthy Web sites. Over the course of a month, I developed into an educated user of the World Wide Web.

I was ready to work with the students—or so I thought.

I installed my Internet software on one of the multimedia computers in the media center. The school custodian moved a phone line near the computer. When a student came to the media center with a research question, we logged on and *tried* to find the answer together. I emphasize "tried" because sometimes we were not successful. Sometimes we used a computer search engine (Yahoo! or Alta Vista) and sometimes we tried to find a Web site in our printed World Wide Web directories.

You have to remember that my students are 11, 12, and 13 years old. Their research assignments are usually quite basic. One student wanted to research "jaguars" (the animal) on the Internet. An Alta Vista search yielded thousands of Web sites, many of which were about the Jaguar automobile. This student, and countless others like him, ended up with the print encyclopedia, happy to have their information yet disappointed at their Internet experience.

Then one day it all clicked. A young lady was part of a student team working on a report about Ireland. She wanted to research Irish dancing. The card catalog indicated that I had no books in the collection about Irish dancing, and the encyclopedia contained only passing references. This girl wanted to learn about the dances, their origins, the costumes, and all of the tradition. We logged on to the Internet and searched for "Irish dancing." Within a few minutes, we found a Web site that had all of the information she needed. We hit the print button.

Over the next couple of months similar experiences led me to two conclusions:

1. There is useful information about many topics on the Internet. Material on small and obscure topics can now be easily accessed. My media center just got a whole lot bigger.

2. Finding information on the Internet is a two-pronged task: finding the correct Web sites and then finding the information within the Web site.

I think the first prong—finding the Web sites—must be learned first-hand, or at least taught on a one-to-one basis. Most of the time you can't know if a Web site meets your needs until you access it. However, with practice you can become skillful at looking at a list of search results and selecting the best possibilities. The second prong—finding the information within a Web site, is also best experienced first-hand. The best practice comes when students are given the Web site and told what to find; in essence, a World Wide Web scavenger hunt. Both teachers and students can benefit from a collection of ready-made World Wide Web exercises. This book, *Wading the World Wide Web*, addresses this need.

To some, I'm sure this approach will seem overly formal and restrictive. "Isn't the beauty of the Web the ability to jump from site to site, 'surfing' all around the world?" you say.

My response: you're absolutely right. But these are two different tasks. It's the difference between catching a fish and cooking a fish; the difference between growing a head of lettuce and preparing a salad. In both of these rather contrived illustrations, the former task involves acquiring the raw materials, and the latter converting those materials into something useful. Both tasks are useful—even critical to the process. But they are different activities. "Surfing the Web" can be very confusing to someone who doesn't know how to swim. That's why this book is called *Wading the World Wide Web*.

I'm not sure why "surfing" was chosen as a moniker for hypertext jumping. I tried to surf in the ocean once. It was a thrilling, stimulating, physical experience. Don't get the wrong impression—I failed miserably at surfing. I hit my head on the surfboard, drank about a gallon of seawater, and scraped my face on the sandy bottom. I've searched the Internet hundreds of times, and I've never seen anything as beautiful as the ocean, or had an experience as exhilarating as being on a narrow board zipping through the water. But I guess surfing and "surfing the Net" do have some things in common: using the Internet can be frustrating, and sometimes you feel like you've been hit in the head with a board.

In both situations, it's very easy for beginners to get in over their heads.

So why do we forestall the excitement of surfing the Net and "wade" instead? Here are six reasons:

- Wading gives students an entry-level Internet experience. Just like wading in the ocean, it's a way to get your students' feet wet without taking them too far from the shore.

- Wading teaches students to spend time on each Web page. Remember those Viewmaster toys we had as children? Each reel showed a series of three-dimensional scenes. All of the reels were captioned, and some were even accompanied by their own storybooks. Yet how often did we spend on each reel? Click ... click ... click ... click ... click ... next reel—just long enough to see each picture. Some people use their TV remotes the same way. (We usually think of channel-surfing as negative and wasteful, but Web-surfing as positive and educational.) Stay on each channel just long enough to get an image, then move on. The exercises in this book require students to appreciate each Web page they encounter before "flipping the channel."

- Wading activities emphasize the information value of the World Wide Web. Sure, many of your students know about the Web, but what do they *really* know? Most teenagers can find video game sites and chat rooms, but very few students are aware of the information available on the World Wide Web.

- Wading teaches the strengths of the World Wide Web. Each of the Web sites used in the activities section was selected to display the strong points of the World Wide Web.
- Wading shows examples of well-designed Web sites. By viewing several of these excellent sites, your students will become sophisticated users of the World Wide Web. They will soon see the difference between high-quality sites and pretenders.
- Wading gives beginners a sense of accomplishment. Using the World Wide Web for the first time can be confusing and frustrating. By following the plans and sending your students to specific sites to find answers to assigned questions, you can almost guarantee a successful beginning experience.

Using This Book

Wading the World Wide Web consists of two parts. The first part contains two brief chapters about the World Wide Web and recommendations for implementing the Web in the school setting. I hope the ideas are useful and thought-provoking.

The second half contains 41 exercises, each with student handouts and a teacher plan, that use World Wide Web sites as resources. Duplication rights for the student handouts are released within your school. In other words, if Lewis Middle School buys this book, then its staff can photocopy the student handouts for use by the students in that school.

A Note About the Web Sites

At last count, there were over 16 million sites on the World Wide Web. It was very difficult to select the Web sites on which to base the exercises. No sites were purposefully ignored; no racial, political, or other groups were favored or discriminated against. Web sites were selected using five basic criteria:

1. They are high-quality Web sites, following the criteria described in chapter 1 of this book.
2. They have educational value.
3. They offer free, unregistered access to students.
4. They cover topics that students find interesting.

5. They are relatively stable; in other words, they should continue to provide useful information long after this book is published.

A Final Note

The World Wide Web is a volatile medium. Excellent Web sites can move, change focus, or completely disappear overnight. Anyone who uses the Web can affirm this characteristic. High-quality Web sites can be expensive and time-consuming to maintain. Sometimes companies or organizations cannot bear this expense. If any of these Web sites changes drastically or disappears before you get a chance to use the exercise, please accept my apologies. The table of contents has undergone several revisions since the inception of this book in an effort to provide the most stable Web sites. If you find that one has disappeared, visit my support site at **http://www.schooltv.com/wading.htm**, where you'll find updates and new exercises that are current to the moment.

If we waited for Web sites to stop changing, this book would never be finished.

And isn't that really the strength of the World Wide Web?

1 Understanding the World Wide Web

Welcome to the World Wide Web!

The idea of connecting a classroom computer to thousands of other computers around the world solicits a myriad of responses from today's educators. Many teachers are excited about the opportunity to access information from other cities, states, and nations. Others are interested in downloading graphics and audio clips to support their daily lessons. Still more educators are reworking assignments and instructional units around newfound educational resources.

Unfortunately, a large number of educators face this new tool with apprehension, reticence, and fear. And who can blame them? When most teachers received their college degrees, the concept of a World Wide Web was merely a glimmer in the eye of a British physicist. The authors of Mosaic and Netscape are young enough to be remembered as students, not communications pioneers. Back then, "buying hardware" meant nails, hammers, and plumbing supplies purchased from the corner store, and software—well, software wasn't even a word. The thought of trashing a file cabinet full of handouts and lesson plans is scary. Some teachers even feel betrayed. "No one told me that we'd have to learn all of this," exclaimed a career teacher at a recent inservice meeting. Truly, many educators didn't envision the technology-equipped classroom when they decided to enter the teaching field. I cannot imagine a career that has changed in such a fundamental way as education in general and media education specifically.

But technology is upon us, ready or not. Whether the educator is poised to learn and embrace new developments or reluctant to investigate the medium's possibilities, a working knowledge of the technology is usually helpful to understanding its use in the educational setting. Although not intended to be an exhaustive discussion of all aspects of the World Wide Web, this chapter will give you a good background. First, we'll learn a brief history of the World Wide Web. Then we'll discuss the hardware, software, and communications connections needed to access the Web.

In the second half of this chapter, we'll examine the resources available on the Web. First we'll look at some characteristics common to most Web pages. Then we'll learn how to find the Web sites that will help us in the curriculum area. Finally, we'll discuss some evaluative criteria for these Web sites.

So, welcome to the World Wide Web. It's okay if you're a little bit scared. Just don't let that fear stand between your students and a world of information that will undoubtedly help them in their educational journeys.

The Nature of the World Wide Web

Has any technology so quickly grasped the interest and imagination of the world as the Internet, and its most popular feature, the World Wide Web? Even if you're not a regular Web user, it's impossible to escape the incredible influence of this relatively new medium. Words like "online" and "connected" have taken on new meaning. Almost every advertisement and news program invites viewers to log on and learn more. Electronic mail has revolutionized personal communication. A wealth of valuable information can be accessed at a computer keyboard. Remember when they told us that one day we would have 500 television channels? Well, this is it! Except the screen belongs to the computer, and they were off by about 16 million channels.

But how did the World Wide Web get so big so fast? Part of the answer comes from the history of the Web.

A Brief History of the World Wide Web

The World Wide Web, like its precursor the Internet, developed in an arena that doesn't get much attention, the academic community. In 1989, George Bush was beginning his term as president. "Rain Man" and "Field of Dreams" were box office hits. Oliver North was testifying before Congress, and the Exxon Valdez spilled 240,000 barrels of oil in Prince William Sound. The Internet had been in limited yet healthy use for 20 years, riding the backbone of the federal government's ARPANET, and later the National Science

Foundation's NSFNET. Communication consisted mainly of academics and researchers sending electronic mail, uploading and downloading files, and posting messages to online discussion groups. The Internet was a valuable resource for information, but it lacked the high-concept, exciting, "wow" characteristics of television and motion pictures.

Meanwhile, British physicist Tim Berners-Lee was in his fifth year working on the data acquisitions systems of CERN, the European Particle Physics Lab in Geneva, Switzerland. Tim's job was to gather data and make it available for researchers working across the European Community. In March of 1989, Berners-Lee began circulating "Information Management: A Proposal," a paper he had written that proposed a system of "distributed computing" among the members of CERN. The project was supported by a software program called ENQUIRE, which he had written for his personal use but never published. ENQUIRE allowed the user to link documents together and jump from one document to another, and then back again. Berners-Lee found this program useful in his own research and saw it as a way to enhance communication and resource sharing among CERN researchers.

By 1990, CERN had become one of the leading Internet servers in Europe. Berners-Lee continued fine-tuning his proposal. Another researcher, Robert Cailliau, joined the efforts, and by October 1990 the basic concepts of the World Wide Web had been established. By the end of the year, a system of communication, Web site construction, and site identification had been developed, and researchers at CERN began using the new system of communication. The World Wide Web allowed a researcher reading a document on a computer screen to quickly jump to related articles without having to perform a complicated computer search. More information was just a mouse-click away. The researchers began using Berners-Lee's program to write their documents and add these connecting links. Resource sharing and research at CERN became much more efficient.

During the summer of 1991, CERN became an active promoter of the new World Wide Web. It hosted a World Wide Web seminar in June and appointed additional researchers to the project to help Berners-Lee achieve his vision. By December, CERN was ready to share the project with the world. It presented the World Wide Web at the "Hypertext '91" conference in San Antonio, Texas, and elaborated on the project in its popular computer newsletter. In early 1992, a rudimentary browser was released for free download over the Internet, making hypertext available to everyone. CERN continued the publicity with demonstrations in France, Austria, Germany, and the United States.

By January 1993, more than 50 computer servers were using the CERN World Wide Web technology, allowing users to instantly access information around the world. In March 1993, the World Wide Web accounted for 0.1 percent of NSFNET Internet traffic; by September, the figure had increased tenfold. By October, more than 200 servers were available.

Although World Wide Web progress may have seemed a bit Eurocentric at this point, the Americans were not ignoring the phenomenon. The National Center for Supercomputing Applications (NCSA) at the University of Illinois at Urbana-Champagne was working on a project to make the Web more user-friendly. Their idea was to build on the CERN World Wide Web/hypertext concept, and add graphics, photographs, and sounds to the package (remember, the CERN concept centered around text and data, not entertainment).

Marc Andreessen was an undergraduate student at the university, earning $6.85 an hour to write software for the NCSA. He was supposed to be working on a 3-D visualization program, but was more interested in the World Wide Web. Andreessen, along with a handful of his peers, worked for three months developing Mosaic, the user-friendly Internet browsing tool that their university computing center had envisioned. Mosaic was a smash success! The university gave the program to anyone who wanted it, and Andreessen became a hero to the Internet world. Now, Web page authors could add graphics, sounds, pictures, and animations to their Web sites. The World Wide Web grew by leaps and bounds. By the end of 1993, more than 2 million Web pages were on the World Wide Web.

In early 1994, Andreessen received an e-mail message from Jim Clark, founder of Silicon Graphics. Clark's message was simple—use Clark's capital and business experience and Andreessen's talent in software authoring to further develop Internet software products. Andreessen and a few other programmers left NCSA in March 1994 to form Mosaic Communications with Clark. NCSA was none too pleased at Clark and Andreessen's decision to use the Mosaic name. By the end of the year, Mosaic Communications had changed its name to Netscape and had begun developing its own browser software, the Netscape Navigator.

In 1994 World Wide Web development was fast and furious. Early in the year, Spry Technology marketed its "Internet in a Box," a collection of software programs (including the SPRY version of Mosaic) designed to connect the home computer market to the World Wide Web. Later that spring, NCSA sold the patents and commercial licensing rights to the original Mosaic software to Spyglass, Inc., which briefly controlled the browser marketplace. Ironically, Marc Andreessen's biggest competitor was selling a product that Andreessen himself had created. (Spyglass now focuses more on developing business applications for the World Wide Web.) Not to be outdone, Netscape offered the first version of its browser, Navigator, free as an Internet download. Users were invited to openly comment on Navigator and make suggestions, further elevating Andreessen's mythic status as a software designer for the people (all before his 24th birthday!). Navigator 1.0 was released to the public in December 1994, with a selling price of $39. The software remained (and still remains) a free download for academic and nonprofit use.

CERN continued to develop the World Wide Web in Europe. It hosted the First International WWW Conference in May 1994. Four hundred delegates attended and at least that many more had to be turned away. The Second International WWW Conference was held five months later in Chicago. Two thousand computer enthusiasts applied for the 1,300 spaces.

In July 1994, the Massachusetts Institute of Technology (MIT) and CERN agreed to found the W3 Organization to guide future development of the World Wide Web. W3 held its first meeting at MIT (Cambridge) that December. Tim Berners-Lee, the original World Wide Web visionary, was named director. The World Wide Web had doubled in size during 1994.

Recent World Wide Web developments involved business more than technological developments. Software giant Microsoft had decided to enter the browser market. Microsoft's Internet Explorer was included with the new Windows 95 operating system. Unlike Netscape, Microsoft provides Internet connection service as well as browser software. The Microsoft Web sites are heavily promoted on the NBC and MSNBC television networks. At the time of this writing, Microsoft Internet Explorer is chipping away at Netscape's once-dominant share of the browser market. Late in 1995, Netscape decided to go public, raising capital by offering stock for sale. The stock opened at $71 a share, making Netscape founders Clark and Andreessen instant millionaires, even though Netscape had yet to show a profit. (Today, Andreessen's stock is valued at more than $130 million; Clark's at more than $1 billion.) Andreessen was featured on the cover of TIME magazine in February 1996. The article, titled "High Stakes Winners," featured Andreessen and other young technology millionaires.

The Internet doubled in size again in 1995, with almost 10 million registered Web sites, and showed 16 million sites on the books by January 1997. The Internet continues to grow at a breakneck pace, with a new Web page being posted every 30 seconds.

Now we can honestly say that the world is in a World Wide Web frenzy. Each day, millions of people use the World Wide Web.

It may be scary, but at least you're not alone.

Computer Hardware Needed to Access the World Wide Web

A good computer is essential if you're going to use the World Wide Web. Fortunately, almost all new computers on the market today meet the criteria demanded. Also, many older computers can easily be upgraded to allow full World Wide Web access.

The Computer System

When choosing a computer to access the World Wide Web, remember: faster is better. Most World Wide Web users will become frustrated if they have to wait more that a few seconds for each page to load. Other than the actual telephone line connection (which will be discussed later in this section), factors that affect computer/World Wide Web performance are processor, RAM, and hard drive space.

Processor

Your computer's processor will determine the speed at which the computer can process the information being sent over the telephone line. For IBM-compatible systems, a 486 DX2-66 represents the lowest acceptable level for moderately quick World Wide Web access. Many schools are upgrading all designated Internet computers to at least the Pentium 75 or a 686 P133 processor. At the time of this writing, most new computers are equipped with a Pentium 266 or 686-266 processor.

An Apple LC or Performa is capable of navigating the World Wide Web, but a Macintosh or Power Mac is probably better suited to the task.

Random Access Memory (RAM)

RAM represents the amount of data that the computer can access at one time. When computing demands exceed that measurement, your computer must begin to used hard-drive space and/or dump information from RAM to make way for the new information. Eight megabytes (8 MB) of RAM is required for most modern browser software. Most schools are upgrading their computers to at least 16 megabytes of RAM. In new computers, 32 megabytes and even 64 megabytes are commonplace. When purchasing computers for World Wide Web access, make sure that you can add additional RAM in the future. RAM modules are inexpensive (less than $200 for 64 additional megabytes) and easily installed by someone with minimal hardware experience. If your computer allows the addition of RAM, an older 4-megabyte computer can be upgraded to 64 megabytes for a small investment.

Hard Drive

World Wide Web browser software saves (caches) the last few Web sites visited on the hard drive. Therefore, empty hard drive space is required. As a rule of thumb, anytime your hard drive is left with only 100 megabytes of empty space, consider investing in a new hard drive, or at least delete unwanted data on the hard drive. Newer computers are equipped with 4-gigabyte (4,000-megabyte) or 6-gigabyte (6,000-megabyte) hard drives.

Modem

The modem converts the analog telephone signals into digital signals that your computer can process. Modem speed is measured in bits per second (BPS). A modem speed of at least 28,800 BPS (also known as 28.8 KBPS) should be used to access the World Wide Web. New computers are usually equipped with 33.6 KBPS or 56 KBPS modems. A new modem can be purchased for about $150.

Graphics

Your computer's graphics capability is a function of the graphics card inside the computer, and the computer monitor itself. Your computer should be able to produce at least 256 colors, known as VGA graphics. This standard has been the minimum for many years. New computers are able to produce millions of colors. However, when using the World Wide Web, it may be beneficial to set your computer to the 256-color setting. This sacrifice will enable Web pages to load faster, and probably won't be noticeable to the eye.

Although a large monitor is not necessary for World Wide Web access, it is nice in the school setting, when more than one student may need to work from the same computer screen. Consider purchasing 17-inch monitors for educational use.

Sound Card and Speakers

Many Web sites include audio information. A computer sound card will allow you to download the audio portion of these Web sites, which can be heard over amplified speakers attached to your computer. Most sound cards are compatible with industry leader Sound Blaster or lesser-known IBM competitor M-Wave.

Printer

Most World Wide Web users will desire a hard copy of information that they find. A good ink-jet printer that can be purchased for $200 to $300 will serve this need.

Upgrading versus Buying

Most schools have an assortment of older computers that fall short of the minimum criteria described previously. Before upgrading your older computers, consider the price of a new computer system. Here's an example: a school wants to upgrade a 486-SX25 computer (vintage 1992) with 4 meg of

RAM, a 4,800 BPS modem, and a 400-megabyte hard drive, which is full. A new processor (chip and motherboard) to upgrade the system to a Pentium 200 would cost about $600. Thirty-two megabytes of RAM would sell for about $200. A 56 KBPS modem costs around $150. A new 4-gigabyte hard drive costs $250. Our total so far is $1,200, not including installation costs. A new system with a full-year warranty could be purchased for about the same price, including a new mouse, sound card, video card, and keyboard. Become an informed consumer before deciding to upgrade older machines.

Of course, that 486 SX-25 could continue to provide excellent service in many computer applications, including word processing, data management, and spreadsheet applications. A computer doesn't have to be World Wide Web-ready to be useful in the school setting.

Computer Software Needed to Access the World Wide Web

World Wide Web software programs allow the computer user to process the information entering the computer through the modem. Without these programs, the World Wide Web would be that scratchy, squealing computer noise that you hear when you first log on. Two types of software used are Web browsers and plug-ins.

Web Browsers

Earlier in this chapter, we looked at the history of the World Wide Web. Although Tim Berners-Lee invented the World Wide Web, it was Marc Andreessen and his cohorts at NCSA who developed the first graphics-based Web browser, Mosaic. A *Web browser* is a software program that allows a computer user to navigate the World Wide Web.

Competing Web Browsers

Currently, two Web browsers dominate World Wide Web computing. They are Netscape Navigator (Marc Andreessen, Jim Clark and company) and Microsoft Internet Explorer (Bill Gates). Mosaic (now administered by Spyglass) is among the few lesser-used browsers.

Although these Web browser programs differ in name and ownership, they are remarkably similar. Most of their features are about the same; some are merely renamed. Netscape and Microsoft continuously update their browsers, but the upgrades are parallel. Most World Wide Web users can use either system. Neither system has gained a technological edge thus far.

Both Netscape Navigator and Microsoft Internet Explorer are readily available for purchase. Netscape Navigator can be downloaded from the Netscape Web site. Microsoft Internet Explorer is included as part of Windows 95 (and future Windows incarnations). Check with your Internet provider before purchasing or downloading this product. Most providers (like Sprint or America Online) provide one of these programs free when you sign up for service. (Service providers are discussed later in this chapter.)

Web Browser Features

A Web browser allows a user to "navigate" the World Wide Web. Several features facilitate this exploration:

- A blank that allows direct typing of known Internet addresses, such as **http://www.lu.com** (the Libraries Unlimited Web site).
- A direct link to electronic mail (e-mail) functions.
- A way to bookmark your favorite Web sites, so that they may be accessed with a simple point-and-click.
- On-screen buttons that let you go back to previous Web pages (and return). This also prevents the chore of retyping Internet addresses.
- A way of printing Web pages and downloading files.
- A procedure for changing display characteristics (font size, colors, etc.)
- The ability to use plug-ins, which are described in the next section.

Most browsers also provide single-click access to their own corporate Web sites so the user can view "help" screens and learn more about their products.

Plug-Ins

Plug-ins are software programs that enhance the operation of your Web browser. As the name describes, a plug-in runs alongside the Web browser and is used when World Wide Web information demands. Plug-in programs may be required when the user wants to hear audio clips, view video segments, access animated Web sites, and participate in chat sessions.

Some of the more popular plug-ins are available for purchase at computer software stores or through mail-order software vendors. Usually, plug-ins can be downloaded directly from the World Wide Web. The company that markets the plug-in will have its own Web site. A computer user can download (copy over the phone line via modem) the plug-in for use with his or her Web browser. After an evaluation period (usually 30 days), the user is required to register the plug-in and mail payment to the vendor. Plug-ins are usually inexpensive; many are free.

When a user encounters a Web site that requires a plug-in, the Web browser posts such a message on the computer screen. The message usually reads, "This Web site requires the Brand X plug-in. Do you want to get this plug-in now?" The user can click the "Yes" button to go directly to the plug-in Web site for the download. If the user chooses "No," he or she can probably continue to use the Web site in question, but will not be able to fully access the areas that require the plug-in.

Internet Providers

You have probably heard the phrases "The Internet is free!" and "No one owns the World Wide Web!" If this is so, then why do we have to pay a monthly service fee to use the Internet?

The Internet *is* free, but it isn't accessible through the normal telephone system. To access the Internet and the World Wide Web, you must go through some type of Internet service provider (ISP). In addition to Internet access, the ISP will probably provide Web browser software, an e-mail account, and technical support. Some ISPs offer hard-drive space on their main computer for subscribers to post their own personal Web pages.

In the early days of the World Wide Web (i.e., a couple of years ago), most ISPs counted the hours each of the subscribers spent online, and billed on an hourly basis. Now, most ISPs provide unlimited service for a flat monthly fee (usually around $20). When selecting an ISP, make sure that (1) the dial-up phone number is a local call, and (2) you know the payment structure. Internet access really isn't very expensive, but hourly rate plans and out-of-area telephone charges can increase access costs exponentially.

ISPs can be categorized as local access providers, national access providers, and full-service providers.

Local Access Providers

In most cities and towns across America, you can see a local Internet access provider nestled in between the dry cleaner and the bookstore. Providing Internet access has become a profitable small business. The local access provider has a multiline telephone system connected to a computer server. The server is directly connected to the Internet. Local residents subscribe to the Internet service by visiting this local business. They are given the dial-up phone number, a password, and perhaps a copy of Web browsing software. At their homes or offices they dial the phone number, type in the password, and launch the Web browser.

Many computer users like the personal service provided by local access providers. They will probably get to know the provider on a first-name basis, and can stop by the business for technical advice. Many local access providers also sell computers, software, and computing books. They may even offer computer repair service, including updating modems and hardware. Local access providers frequently offer an "Internet Café," an area in the store where a potential user can use an Internet-connected computer while enjoying a beverage or snack.

Using a local access provider can have its drawbacks. If a local provider becomes quite popular in the community, it may not have enough phone lines to service all its registered users. This may result in log-in delays or busy signals. The small business may not be able to invest funds in equipment upgrades, as the owner is depending on the profits to put food on his or her table. A breakdown of the local provider's phone system or computer server may mean that the users are without access for a time. Finally, many small businesses do not succeed. What happens when the electric and phone companies disconnect your local provider and creditors repossess the equipment? What happens to e-mail messages that were never delivered? Carefully weigh the advantages and disadvantages of using a local provider.

National Access Providers

National companies also provide Internet access. They generally offer the same service as the local providers, but they are owned and operated by larger companies. Sprint and AT&T are national access providers. Customers hear about these services through television, magazines, or direct-mail advertising. Software, registration, and technical support are handled over the telephone and by mail, as these providers do not have local storefronts. Internet traffic is often routed through existing telephone company computers, making these services extremely dependable. If one system breaks, another quickly takes its place. Services can be rerouted over different phone lines in case of extended outages.

In choosing a national access provider, the subscriber loses the personal dimension offered by the local provider, but gains an established, dependable provider. Customers who have some experience on the Internet and don't need face-to-face technical support would benefit from using a national provider.

Full-Service Providers

Some companies provide access to additional, proprietary information as well as Internet access. Stock-market quotes, baseball scores, and weather forecasts can be accessed by using these services and sidestepping the World Wide Web. These are full-service providers. They sell information as well as Internet access. America Online, CompuServe, and Prodigy are the most commonly known full-service providers.

Even though many people use "America Online" as a synonym for the World Wide Web, full-service businesses were developed as an alternative to the Internet of the early 1990s. Teams of employees gather data from a myriad of sources and continuously update these services. A user didn't need to access the World Wide Web; all of the information was available from America Online and its competitors. However, as the Web developed and user demands increased, full-service providers realized that they couldn't continue adding new categories of information. In 1994, these providers began offering World Wide Web access as a part of their service.

There are certainly advantages to using full-service providers. Starting the service is simple. Most users have received a stack of start-up disks in the mail that facilitate the first connection. The proprietary information is plentiful and excellent—no reason to go on the Web for sports results or weather forecasts. Chat rooms are pervasive on many of these services, with celebrity chats available each day. Subscribers can also maintain several user names and e-mail addresses to serve each member of the family. World Wide Web access is available, too.

Full-service providers are not without disadvantages. Because of heavy marketing, millions of people subscribe to these services. This saturation can lead to busy signals and data slowdowns. Customer service can involve a lengthy wait, and discontinuing the service requires patience and perseverance.

From an educational standpoint, full-service providers can present obstacles to learning about the World Wide Web. Students with full-service access (and so much proprietary information available) will see no reason to explore the World Wide Web. In fact, many students with full-service providers at home are quite proficient on America Online, but have never been on the World Wide Web. Chat rooms can be destructive in the educational setting. Because their marketing is aimed at the home computer user, full-service providers emphasize entertainment over information. This focus is often counterproductive in the educational setting, and misleads students concerning the information available on the World Wide Web.

Carefully evaluate your needs before selecting an Internet service provider. The decision will dramatically affect the service that you can provide your faculty and students.

Communications Connections

The Modem Connection

If you choose from the Internet service providers described earlier, you'll be using a standard modem connection. A *modem* is a computer device that

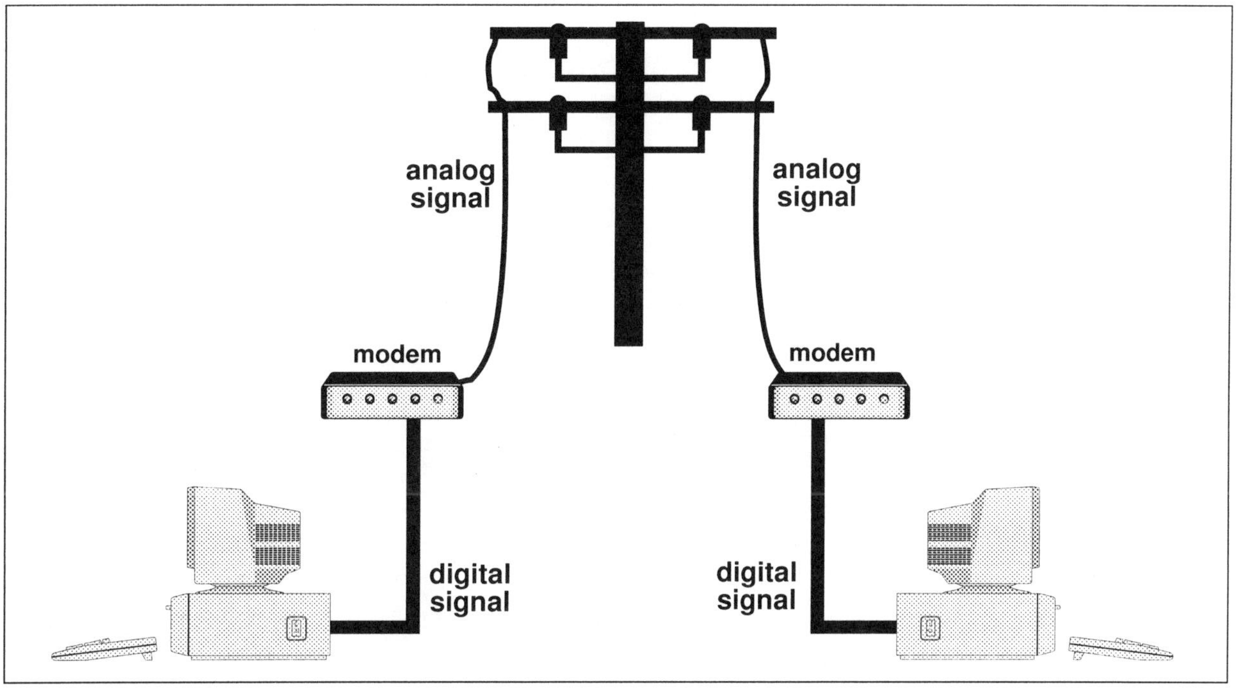

Figure 1.1 Function of a modem.

modulates the analog telephone signal into a digital signal that your computer can use (see fig. 1.1). Outgoing digital signals are demodulated, converting them into analog signals that a standard telephone line can carry. That's where the name "modem" originated, as an abbreviation of "modulator/demodulator." A modem is the most common way that individuals connect to the World Wide Web.

Unfortunately, telephone lines are not designed to facilitate high-speed communications. In fact, the telephone technology used in your house is about the same as it was before the home computer was developed. The phone line is the weak link in the connection between the computer user and the World Wide Web. At best, a regular analog phone line can handle 33,600 BPS (or 33.6 KBPS). Most new computers come with a 33.6 or 56 KBPS modem installed. Slower modems are available, but not much cheaper. The 33.6 KBPS is considered the minimum standard for moderately quick World Wide Web use.

Modems with speeds of 56,000 BPS (56 KBPS) are now available. But why bother with a modem that performs faster than the capacity of analog phone lines? The key to receiving computer signals at 56 KBPS is subscribing to the Internet using a provider connected to the digital part of the telephone system. This provider sends the signals in an encoded, digital format (instead of the typical analog format), allowing your computer to process the signals at 56 KBPS instead of 33.6 KBPS. Your 56 KBPS modem decodes the signals, resulting in speeds appreciably faster than 33.6 KBPS.

Remember that the speeds mentioned (33.6 KBPS, 56 KBPS) are modem capacities under optimum connection circumstances. Rarely are these top speeds achieved. Internet traffic, both on the World Wide Web and at your ISP, is the main factor affecting actual BPS rates. However, the rates are useful for comparison. Under the same circumstances, a 56 KBPS modem will be faster than a 33.6 KBPS modem.

The single computer/single phone line setup is useful for home and small business users of the Internet. Most small-scale users install a second analog phone line in the home or office, or simply disconnect the telephone and use the single phone line for the Internet. (This is especially useful for Internet users who don't want to be disturbed by telephone calls!)

Of course, the school setting is a different ball game. Most schools would prefer World Wide Web access in most teaching areas, as well as the library media center and the writing lab. There are two ways for schools to use computer/modem technology.

Single Computer

A single computer in a central location could be attached to the phone line. The computer would be connected to the World Wide Web in the morning and remain connected throughout the school day. The computer would probably be stationed in the library media center, and students and faculty members could visit throughout the day. Obviously, this is not the widespread Internet infusion that most schools envision, but it does have its place. This small-scale service is a good introduction to the World Wide Web, especially if a large-scale installation is in the works. For example, a school media specialist has been informed that the district will provide full Internet access to the school in the following school year. The media specialist can procure an additional telephone line in the media center and subscribe to the Internet through an ISP. (Funding to pay the monthly connection fee can come from book fair proceeds, PTA donations, or a special arrangement with the local ISP.) The media specialist can begin to teach students and faculty members about the World Wide Web using this single station in the media center. The media specialist can include World Wide Web in his or her media center orientation lesson and teach basic search strategies. When the next school year begins and the school-wide Internet connection is in place, the students and faculty will already be aware of basic World Wide Web content and search strategies.

Some smaller school media centers and public school libraries may adopt this single-computer approach on a long-term basis. The small Florida city of Valparaiso (population 6,000) has a fine full-service public library. Recently, the Valparaiso Community Library became the first public library in the area to offer free Internet access to its patrons. An extra analog telephone line was installed, a local ISP was contracted, and a new computer was purchased. The total start-up cost was less than $2,000 (computer, printer, computer desk, phone line installation) and the monthly overhead is less than $35 (phone line and Internet access). For a modest investment, the citizens have full Internet access. The librarian reports that the Internet is frequently in use, and serves as a valuable complement to the books, periodicals, and audiovisual materials available for checkout. Valparaiso citizens interested in genealogy are especially enthused about the Internet access at the library. This same approach may work for small schools with light research demands. A small elementary school may find the single-computer model appropriate. Although probably not a long-term solution for providing complete Internet access to a school, a single analog connection is a good option for schools that are still investigating and testing the power and potential of the World Wide Web.

Multiple ISP Connections

Schools may choose to multiply the single-connection approach by providing several ISP connections throughout the school. A small school could provide limited Internet access with as few as five individual connections. Careful planning could allow the faculty to fully utilize this resource. For example, one connection in the library media center and one in each grade level would provide at least a marginal level of access. Obstacles to this method include the need for multiple telephone extensions (does a school ever have enough phone lines?) and the cost of multiple ISP accounts (multiply the number of accounts by $20). Schools may be able to negotiate a discounted fee from a local Internet service provider. Some schools may be able to bypass the ISP completely by using a state-sponsored Internet access provider, like FIRN in Florida, TENET in Texas, or CORE+ in California. Local colleges and universities may also be able to help.

Advanced Internet Connections

For a long-term solution to the challenge of providing Internet access to all learners and faculty, most schools are turning to advanced Internet connection strategies. Many of these options are available now, and more loom just over the horizon. The current options are ISDN, T-1, and cable.

ISDN Connections

An integrated services digital network (ISDN) connection can be thought of as a super-high-speed modem. An ISDN connection can deliver at speeds approaching 128,000 BPS (128 KBPS), or almost four times as fast as the standard 33.6 KBPS connection. However, this speed comes with a hefty price tag. An ISDN converter box must be installed in your school at a cost of up to $400. The phone company will charge about $50 per month for the service, and some phone companies tack on additional per-call charges. An ISDN adapter for your computer (which takes the place of the modem) costs about $250.

Setup can be difficult, and not all ISPs are able to deliver data faster than 56 KPBS. Some ISDN lines allow two or three direct connections instead of the single connection available on an analog phone line. An ISDN can also provide adequate service to a small local area network (LAN) like a school computer network. Videoconferencing and real-time audio and video applications are possible using ISDN technology. Downloads are very fast and Web pages pop on the screen almost instantaneously. ISDN is best used by people with lots of money who want to use the Internet and the World Wide Web without waiting too long for data transmission. For wider access, many schools are relying on other technologies.

T-1 Connections

T-1 lines are fast. Very, very fast. Data transmission rates approach 1,500,000 BPS (1.5 MBPS) or about 11 times faster than the ISDN line. As you can imagine, a T-1 connection can easily provide quick World Wide Web access to more than 100 users. A T-1 connection is a direct data link; no ISP service is required. Although this sounds like the perfect solution for schools, there are, of course, disadvantages. The first is cost: equipment costs can run into the thousands of dollars, and monthly service will cost about $300. The second disadvantage is setup and maintenance. A T-1 system may require the user (the school) to act as an Internet service provider, managing access protocols and e-mail accounts. T-1 is not for the inexperienced, the financially strapped, or the faint-hearted.

But before dismissing T-1 as out of reach for your school, consider the return for the investment. Sure, startup costs are large, but no larger than many other school expenditures. (Many school systems are absorbing T-1 installation costs as a capital improvement in plans that wire the entire school system to the World Wide Web.) The monthly access fee of $300 may seem steep, but compared to 100 ISP subscriptions it represents a real value. As schools begin to demand Internet support, school districts are adding technical support positions to service schools that wish to fully utilize the Internet and the World Wide Web. And because the T-1 line is a separate system, it doesn't monopolize the school's busy switchboard system. At the time of this writing, T-1 technology is the connection of choice for schools wishing to fully integrate the Internet into their programs of instruction.

Cable Connection

You've probably heard of high-definition television (HDTV), the fundamental change in television technology that we can expect within the next few years. HDTV uses a digital signal instead of the current analog RF frequency. Analog TV as we know it will be gradually phased out, and by 2015 will probably disappear altogether. To offer true HDTV, cable TV companies will have to replace existing analog cable with digital cable, probably of the fiber-optic variety. That same cable can carry Internet communications at an astounding rate. In a few years, World Wide Web access may be considered a premium channel. The cable TV industry certainly has the potential of becoming the dominant Internet service provider. Some communities already have Internet access through their cable television companies. The technology allows data transmission of about 30,000,000 BPS (30 MBPS), or about 20 times faster than a T-1 line. But critics point out that this signal will be shared by all television viewers and Internet users on the system, which will undoubtedly result in slowdowns. Cable companies will also have to continuously add and update their facilities to keep up with growing demands. Whatever the case, look for cable TV to make a big impact in the Internet industry within the next few years.

Learning More About the Internet

As stated earlier, this chapter can only begin to explain the intricacies and inner workings of Internet and World Wide Web technology. For some teachers, this simplified overview is enough. Others will want a more in-depth discussion. Fortunately, many resources are available for learning more about this subject. Here are a few that I recommend.

Books

I thoroughly enjoyed *The Internet for Dummies* by Levine, Baroudi, and Young. This is one of those famous yellow-and-black "for dummies" books published by IDG Books Worldwide. The authors have updated their work each year that it has been in publication, and I hope they continue to do so. Although most educators cringe at the title, we can all appreciate the useful information and common-sense approach.

The Internet and Instruction: Activities and Ideas by Barron and Ivers, is published by Libraries Unlimited. It has detailed information about getting your school connected, and I'm sure it will be updated on a regular basis.

Although it's not about the technical side of the World Wide Web, I'm never far from my copy of *The Internet Resource Directory for K-12 Teachers and Librarians*, which was written by Elizabeth Miller, and also published by Libraries Unlimited. One of the best ways to learn about the Web is to look at excellent Web sites, and Miller's list is quite extensive. I can't imagine any media specialist being without a copy.

Visit any bookstore and you'll find several other valuable resources. Just remember, almost every publisher is jumping on the World Wide Web bandwagon. Make sure that you select "you-can" books that will enhance your role as an educator.

Magazines

For excellent, accessible articles, I recommend *PC World*. This magazine regularly features articles about the World Wide Web, and always seems to be on top of recent Internet technological developments.

The first computer magazine that I ever read was *PC Novice*. Now they've changed their name to *Smart Computing in Plain English*. The name change probably helps circulation ("I'll cancel my subscription because I'm not a novice anymore") but the articles remain top-notch and quite user-friendly. Although some articles are very basic, I find a few valuable tips in every issue. This is also a great magazine for students. World Wide Web articles are a staple of almost every issue.

Several magazines are published about surfing the Net, but none compares to *Yahoo! Internet Life*. Sometimes smart, often sassy, but never boring, any issue of *Y!IL* will contain more than 100 Web site reviews on topics as wide-ranging as religion, rap music, and coffee. *Y!IL* never forgets that information is the real reason for the World Wide Web.

Television Shows

A few cable TV networks are producing programs about the World Wide Web. Because cable TV schedules are almost as volatile as the Web itself, recommending specific programs would probably not be productive. But the shows are out there, and we're bound to see more in the future. Here are some networks to check first: CNN, MSNBC, CNBC, and the Sci-Fi Channel.

Educational Conferences

Local, state, and national conferences usually offer sessions about using the World Wide Web in the school setting. Contact your state media organization for a list of conferences. Select workshops that fit your knowledge level and the needs of your learners. Make sure to save a few hours for the exhibit hall, where you'll get the chance to ask vendors about their new products. You may even get a first-hand demonstration!

World Wide Web Resources

Do you know what it's like to produce a nonfiction book? There are many steps between the initial idea and the finished product. Many weeks are spent developing the scope, format, and contents of a book. The manuscript passes the desks of several editors who approve the text and illustrations, copyedit, and typeset the work. Months may pass before you get to hold your bouncing baby book.

I've been through this process several times as an author for Libraries Unlimited. I never really appreciated the process until I started using the World Wide Web. Here are the steps in producing a Web page. Get an idea. Type it into your computer. Upload it onto your ISP's hard drive. This all takes about a half an hour. And the information is available to the entire world, nearly free of charge.

Communications purists applaud the opportunity for expression that the World Wide Web provides to everyone. The Web has even been called "the great equalizer." Now everyone can be published. This is great when considered from the creator's viewpoint, but the audience suffers from this instant, haphazard form of publication.

Here's an example: Recently I was looking for the mailing address of Tiger Direct Software, and I didn't have their catalog handy. I knew they must have a Web site, so I logged on to the Web, accessed a search service, and typed in "Tiger Direct", asking for the first 10 hits. Sure enough, the Tiger Direct Home Page was listed, but I was intrigued by another selection, "Information About Tiger Direct Software." I clicked the link and found myself at a poorly constructed, text-only Web site that had as its banner headline "Tiger Direct Sucks!" This headline was followed by a brief, poorly written essay describing the Web site author's unsuccessful quest for a $10 rebate on some software that he had purchased from this vendor. (I don't think Elizabeth Miller will recommend this Web page in her next *Internet Resource Directory*.)

Anyone who has used the Web extensively can relate a similar story in which they have accessed inaccurate, inflammatory, or useless sites while trying to find accurate, unbiased, useful information. The great equalizer? That's right. "Tiger Direct Sucks!" was right alongside the correct, important information. (For the record, I use Tiger Direct extensively, and have always been a satisfied customer.)

So what's the moral of the story? Simple. Selecting the right Web sites for the educational setting is an important information skill—and it is trickier than teaching students how to find information in the library media center. All school library/media materials have been published by reputable companies that use professional editors. A library media specialist who knows her fellow teachers, her students, and her community has selected each item with great care. Internet resources can be valuable, too. But material that would never be found in a school library media center has equal footing on the Web. And if the World Wide Web is in the media center, then so are those inaccurate, poorly produced Web sites. Remember that shelf of "parent permission only" books that some media specialists have in their media centers? Seems kind of silly now, doesn't it?

In the second half of this chapter, we'll look at the resources available on the World Wide Web. First, we'll describe the anatomy of a Web site and then explore online searching services that will help you find Web sites that meet your needs. To conclude, we'll establish some evaluative criteria to apply to Web sites.

Web site Characteristics

A *Web site* is a collection of one or more Web pages that has been posted on the World Wide Web. Each Web page can be very small (only a few lines of printed text) or quite large. Printed using your printer, a typical Web page would be about five letter-size pages long. Some Web sites consist of 100 or more Web pages, depending on the objectives of the Web site authors and the resources (time and money) they have at their disposal.

HTML, the Language of the World Wide Web

Each Web page is written in a programming language called Hypertext Markup Language (HTML). Using HTML, a Web page creator can indicate the size, font, and location of text, the background colors and patterns, and the graphic images that appear on the Web site. Animations, videos, and sounds are also programmed using HTML. Most users find the HTML code reasonably simple to learn, but there is an even easier option. Programs are available that allow Web page creation using the point/click/drag process used in programs such as CorelDraw and PowerPoint. The programs automatically translate pages that the user has created into HTML documents ready for the World Wide Web. Some of the newer word processing programs offer this option, too. The user simply saves the document as an HTML file, and it is ready to upload onto the Web. These programs help us look to the day when publishing on the World Wide Web becomes as natural as selecting the print button on the computer.

URL, the Web site's Address

But how does your computer know where to look for the Web pages that you would like to see? Each Web site is given a uniform resource locator (URL) when it is posted on the Internet. The URL is the Web site's address on the World Wide Web. The URL is based on several factors, which we'll now explore using the Libraries Unlimited Web site as an example.

http://www.lu.com

The first section of the Web site is known as the *scheme*. The most common scheme is HyperText Transfer Protocol, or http. A colon and two forward slashes follow the scheme.

Next comes the location on the Internet where the Web site can be found. In our example, the Web site is found on the World Wide Web, which is indicated by www. A period (known as a "dot" in Internet jargon) follows the location name.

Next comes the domain name, which is the name of the computer on which the Web site can be found. This first part of the domain name is lu, which is an abbreviation of Libraries Unlimited. (As you may have surmised, the Web site authors could have chosen "librariesunlimited" instead, but that would have been difficult to type.) Savvy Web authors know to make their domain names brief and descriptive.

The second part of the domain name describes the sponsor of the Web site. The sponsor is described using three letters; our Web site uses "com", which is an abbreviation of commercial. These three letters tell the Web site visitor that this Web page is sponsored by a commercial business. "Com" is by far the most common type of Web site. Almost one-fourth of the sites on the World Wide Web are commercial. "Edu" (for educational) is second, with about 16 percent. Nine percent of the sites are "net"—network sites. Other commonly found domain suffixes include:

MIL—United States military

GOV—United States government

ORG—organizations

Most sites located outside the United States bear a simple country abbreviation as their domain suffix. Japan is noted as JP; Germany is DE; Canada is CA. You may be surprised to know that World Wide Web sites are located all over the world. Tonga (TO), Mongolia (MO), and Albania (AL) all have resident Web sites.

Typing the URL takes you to the *home page*, or starting point for the Web site. Most users find the home page helpful when visiting a Web site for the first time. You've probably noticed that when you log on to a Web site and start exploring the different pages, the URLs get longer and longer. That's because you're accessing different pages on that Web site. Part of the

Libraries Unlimited Web site is a page about Teacher Ideas Press, a division of Libraries Unlimited. Information about the Teacher Ideas Press books can be found on **http://www.lu.com**. After the Web site URL, type "/**tip**" to get to the Teacher Ideas Press page.

http://www.lu.com/tip

Many people visit this page every day, but do they type in the "/tip" part themselves? No, they access the Teacher Ideas Press page on the lu Web site by using a hyperlink, which we'll discuss next. However, a World Wide Web user could go directly to the Teacher Ideas Press page by typing the preceding URL, bypassing the Web site home page.

Hyperlinks

Remember why Tim Berners-Lee created the World Wide Web? (Sneak a peek at the beginning of this chapter!) He wanted to link the documents that the CERN researchers were using. Certain words were underlined in each document. By mouse-clicking on one of those words, a user could go immediately to another document explaining that topic. Those selected words and phrases are known as *hyperlinks*. The hyperlink is the major defining feature of the World Wide Web.

Clicking a hyperlink can take the user one of several places, including:

- Another part of the same Web page. A common application takes the visitor to a lower portion of the page. Hyperlinks at the bottom of a Web page may return a user to the top of the page.
- Another page on the same Web site. This technique is commonly used on the Libraries Unlimited Web site, which features a page listing the Libraries Unlimited authors. Each book listing is a hyperlink that takes you to a page on the Libraries Unlimited Web site describing that book.
- Another Web site. Web site authors often provide hyperlinks to other sites of similar interest. In fact, many popular Web sites are simply lists of hyperlinks. The user can bookmark this site and use it as a launching pad to get to several Web sites that share a common theme.
- An e-mail address. Many Web sites feature hyperlinks to e-mail boxes of individuals associated with the Web site. The Web page author almost always has his or her e-mail address hyperlinked. Clubs and organizations often list their officers, with e-mail hyperlinks. Just click the officer's name, and the e-mail function

of your Web browser software appears. E-mail can be composed and immediately sent to the person or organization.

Up to this point, we've discussed hyperlinks in the text sense only, where the user mouse-clicks an underlined or highlighted word on the Web page. However, Web site authors frequently use graphics as hyperlinks. These hyperlinked graphics are known as *image maps,* and they further establish the World Wide Web as a user-friendly communications interface. Each section of the image is "mapped" and serves as a hyperlink. Actual geographic maps make excellent image maps. For example, on a page describing national parks, users can click a state they wish to visit on the image map of the United States. The hyperlink takes the user to a Web page that describes the parks of that state. Other graphical images can be used as image maps too. Users can click on image maps and graphical icons as well as words and phrases on most modern Web sites.

World Wide Web Graphics

As stated earlier, most World Wide Web sites are filled with graphic images. These graphics are usually processed in one of two forms, GIF (graphic interchange format) or JPEG (Joint Photographic Experts Group). Internet service provider CompuServe originated the GIF format as a way to distribute graphics across the many platforms (IBM, Apple, etc.) connected to the Internet. GIFs can handle 256 colors and are used primarily for line drawings. JPEG files support 16.7 million colors (aka "True Color") and are used for photographic-quality images. JPEG files are frequently compressed as they are sent over the Internet, and each compression results in a loss of picture quality. However, the average user doesn't notice the slight loss of quality experienced by accessing the Web page.

Other common graphics formats, such as BMP and PCX, are infrequently used on the World Wide Web. In most cases, these larger, high-quality images must be downloaded; they don't pop up automatically when the Web page is accessed. Although downloading takes time, the result is a clean, crisp image, which is important when the image is to be used in a presentation or in printed form.

Although often visually appealing, graphic-laden Web pages have a downside—the extended time needed to load each page. A home page consisting of a large JPEG image map may take more than a minute to load onto the computer screen. The text-only version would take only a few seconds. Most users would rather see the elaborate graphic, but the time involved (especially when each page on the Web site follows the same graphical pattern) quickly becomes a burden. Web site authors would be wise to use graphics thoughtfully when creating their compositions. Every author should be forced to visit his or her own Web site each week!

Other Visual Considerations

Professional Web pages are designed by graphic artists who are experienced in the concepts of visual literacy. Here are some other factors that determine a Web site's visual impact.

Colors

High- or medium-contrast colors should be used to distinguish background from text. Busy backgrounds are distracting and should be avoided. Black text allows easy content printing. (Have you ever tried to print a page of white text on a black background?)

Fonts

Regardless of the font selected by the Web site author, the user's computer and browser program will determine the size and style of font. For that reason, most Web pages are written using standard fonts (Times New Roman, Arial, etc.) found on most computers. Fancy banner headlines using dynamic fonts are usually created as graphics and saved in the GIF format. This is really the only way to guarantee that an unusual font will be replicated on the visitor's computer.

Frames

Many Web site authors create in the "frames" format. A Web site using this format divides (either vertically or horizontally) the viewing page into two or more separate Web pages. Usually one of the displayed pages contains a table of contents, and the other displayed page contains information about the subject of the Web site. Using the frames format, the visitor always has quick access to the table of contents.

Some users love frames, and others cringe when their selected Web page appears in the frames format. Basically, it's a matter of personal preference. Would you watch two televisions at once (especially if one TV features a graphical *TV Guide*)? If so, then you will probably like frames.

Audio, Video, and Animation Elements

Many Web sites feature audio, video, and animated sequences. Usually the visitor must have the proper plug-in to access these elements (plug-ins are described earlier in this chapter). Animated sequences, which are usually a brief series of GIFs looped together, can be transmitted quickly. Audio and video segments take longer—from several seconds to several minutes. An additional consideration is the value of the audio and/or video being downloaded. You may be willing to endure a several-minute wait to see a video of the Mars Explorer in action. A 30-second welcoming message from a corporate president may not have the same impact.

Downloads

Many Web sites offer the visitor the opportunity to download files. In other words, visitors can copy files from the domain computer onto their computers' hard drives or floppy diskettes. Audio clips, video clips, animations, and documents are frequently available for downloading.

Computer programs (often demonstration versions) are also available for downloading at many Web sites. These files are often transmitted in a compressed format, decreasing the time needed for the download. The user must decompress the file using a special program. (The most common compression format is ZIP.) Naturally, "unzipping" programs are among the most popular Internet downloads. Fortunately, these software "can openers" are available on the Web.

Remember, as technology increases, Web site sophistication will follow. Expect Web sites of the future to offer more opportunities for exploration of the world through the World Wide Web.

Online Searching

Earlier we mentioned the availability of printed Web site directories. Although these directories are useful tools for specialized World Wide Web users, they cannot possibly contain every Web site relevant to the topic of research. Millions of Web pages are available on the Internet, and some sources estimate that 85,000 new pages are being posted every month. That's one new page every 30 seconds! However ambitious and topical, no printed directory can hope to keep track of this dynamic, changing environment. For this reason, online search engines are very popular.

How Do They Work?

Online search engines are Web sites that search and catalog other Web sites. Online search engines explore the World Wide Web using special computer programs called *spiders*. These spider programs determine the topic of each Web site visited and create an index of these results. The result is a large, continuously updated searchable database of Web sites. By typing one or two keywords into the search engine's Web page, you can obtain a list of possibly useful Web sites. Each Web site in the "results" list is hyperlinked to the Web site.

Online Search Engine Disadvantages

Of course, the spider programs can't provide any evaluation of the Web sites they visit. A search for information about dolphins (the marine mammals) will probably garner a few useful sites, but mixed in the list will be sites about dolphin fish (mahi-mahi) recipes, dolphin-shaped jewelry, *The Island of the Blue Dolphins*, and the Miami Dolphins football team. Fortunately, most of these online search engines also provide the first few words of each Web site on the search results screen, so that the user can quickly eliminate Web sites that are completely off the topic.

Another disadvantage of these engines is the amount of time needed for a new Web site to be listed. With the World Wide Web growing exponentially, it may be weeks or even months before the spider programs find and index a new Web site. For example, suppose you are interested in finding out about technology conferences in your state. You access a search engine Web site and type in "Florida + technology + conference" in the search field. (Most online search engines use some form of Boolean searching, but the best strategy varies from site to site. Consult the search engine's "help" screen for the best searching strategy.) The search engine may return "NO RESULTS FOUND." You know that your state hosts several technology conferences each year, and you're sure that those conferences maintain Web sites to inform educators about conference details. Why no results? Probably because the searching spider hasn't found the site yet. Another reason could be that all three search words ("Florida", "technology", and "conference") weren't used in the first 100 words of the Web site (the index range of many of the spider programs). Of course, savvy Web site authors know to put several possible keywords early in their Web site to prevent such searching mishaps. And most organizations have learned to widely publicize the URLs of Web sites of interest to their members. Finally, many online search engines offer the option of submitting your site directly to their database, instead of waiting for a visit from the spider program. Just remember, online search engines are useful, but not perfect.

The Online Directory

Certainly there has to be a more accurate way of finding Web sites—one that eliminates poor-quality sites and off-topic results. The answer is a type of online search engine called an *online directory*. A typical online search engine is an index of Web sites, but a directory is like a table of contents to the World Wide Web. Directories offer the same keyword search options as regular search engines, but they also offer topical guides to subjects of interest. Let's imagine that my friend Chris, who is a big football fan, wants to learn more about his favorite team, the Miami Dolphins. His visit to an online search directory might go like this:

- From the master list, he selects "Recreation and Sports."
- From the "Recreation and Sports" menu, he selects "football."
- From the "football" menu, he selects "professional football teams."
- From the "professional football teams" menu, he selects "Miami Dolphins."

At that point, he receives a list of Web sites about the professional football team, the Miami Dolphins. By clicking on the supplied hyperlinks, he can visit one or all of these Web sites.

Most online search engines integrate some sort of directory option into their services. Other search engines offer on-screen hyperlinks to their affiliated directory sites. As World Wide Web users become more demanding and sophisticated, expect the directory to emerge as the preferred method of online searching.

Accessing Online Search Engines and Directories

Finding online search engines and directories is actually a simple task. Both Netscape Navigator and Microsoft Internet Explorer have one-click links to the most popular search engines. But if you're using another browser program, or you're the sort who likes to type in URLs, here's a list of popular search engines/directories.

- Yahoo!—Yahoo! is a true directory, with thousands of topics and subtopics available. Users can also perform keyword searches that lead not only to Web sites, but to topic listings as well. This is a great place to look if you want to learn more about any topic. Theoretically, sites listed on Yahoo! have been evaluated and deemed worthy by humans. You be the judge. **http://www.yahoo.com**
- Alta Vista—Alta Vista is a huge online search engine, with more than 30 million accessible results. Expect your search to result in thousands of Web sites. That's one busy spider! **http://www.altavista.digital.com**
- Infoseek—Infoseek is a hybrid site; basically a keyword-based search that offers directories as well as search results. Infoseek also features direct links to useful "seeking" Web sites, if you're

looking for a business address, or just curious to see if that old flame is online. **http://www.infoseek.com**

- Lycos—Lycos is a large index of sites, some of which are "rated." Users can select to see only the "top 5%" as rated by Lycos. With such a huge index, that's the recommended strategy. **http://www.lycos.com**

Other popular search sites include:

- Magellan, **http://www.mckinley.com**
- Hot Bot, **http://www.hotbot.com**
- Net Gurus Search Page, **http://net.gurus.com/search**. Not a search engine itself, but a menu of several search engines including "Savvy Search," which combines the results of several search engines. This site is provided courtesy of the authors of *The Internet for Dummies*.

And Now, a Word from Our Sponsor ...

How much does it cost to use an online search engine? Absolutely nothing! That's because each page on the search engine includes a colorful advertisement. These advertisements are almost always hyperlinked to Web sites that tell you more about the product or service. Many times, the advertisement is directly related to your search results. For example, if you use a search engine to find information about automobile tires, an advertisement for a tire manufacturer will likely appear on the results page. A single click takes you to that page. Many companies advertise on the World Wide Web. Advertising on search engines is another way for their messages to reach an audience.

Evaluating Web sites

Many of the criteria that media educators apply to books, computer software, and audiovisual recordings can also be used to evaluate Web sites. However, because Web sites can be "published" by anyone with a computer, it is important for educators to apply these criteria consistently to offer reliable, accurate resources for students. The following criteria are offered as a starting point for the evaluation of World Wide Web sites.

Accuracy

Web sites should offer consistently accurate information. When possible, use other media (encyclopedia, CD-ROM, etc.) to verify the accuracy of information on Web sites with which you have no experience. Inaccurate information indicates that the Web site authors are not fully committed to designing a useful resource.

Authority

Determine the credentials of the author or organization sponsoring the Web site. Web sites sponsored by educational facilities (.edu) and government agencies (.gov) can be expected to adhere to the standards of their institutions. Sites sponsored by businesses (.com) and organizations (.org) answer only to their own standards. The author of a book or print encyclopedia article about a certain topic is probably an expert in his or her field. An independent Web site author may lack qualifications for expert status in other media that have more stringent requirements for publication.

Intent and Motivation

Closely related to authority, this criterion speaks to the issues of economics and influence. Unlike a public or school library, the World Wide Web is a place of business as well as a storehouse of information. Although commercial (.com) sites can offer useful information, the desired result is for the user to spend money with the Web site's sponsor.

Many sites sponsored by nonprofit organizations seek to influence public opinion. This practice is not inherently deceptive. However, propaganda abounds on the World Wide Web, so educators must carefully evaluate the motives and reputations of organizations offering information over the Internet. Opinion on the World Wide Web is not always clearly labeled as such.

Depth

A Web site should offer more than a cursory explanation of any topic. A single paragraph of text reflects the effort of a hobbyist, not an expert. Although multipage documents are not required, they often reflect the thoroughness necessary for many topics.

Scope

Does the Web page adequately cover the topic? Some Web pages are attractive, but offer information that could be found in a child's picture book. A useful Web site should provide information that satisfies the research needs of the user.

Currency

Is the Web page updated periodically? One of the most powerful aspects of the World Wide Web is the ability of authors to update their Web sites frequently. Surprisingly, many otherwise excellent sites have become hopelessly out of date. Web sites dealing with current event topics should be updated as those events develop.

Stability

Change is not a virtue. Web sites that continue to offer valuable information should not change at the whim of the author. A Web site that changes only for the sake of change can present a confusing challenge for a repeat visitor. This is the equivalent of moving the library shelves each month. Regular patrons will be unable to browse their favorite sections and new visitors won't notice any improvement. Unless the information changes, a stable site is desirable.

Visual Style

Web sites should offer text that is easy to read on a background that provides contrast and doesn't strain the eyes. Chartreuse text on a psychedelic background may impress a few close friends, but will likely frustrate Web site visitors seeking useful information. A simple, direct design is usually the best approach for communicating over the World Wide Web.

Thoughtful Hyperlink Design

The ability to hyperlink Web sites is one of the defining features of the World Wide Web. Excellent sites realize this potential; poor sites do not. A good Web site provides links to other Web pages related to the topic. Links should also take the user to other pages within the site, including the site's home page.

The presentation of hyperlinks is just as important as their inclusion. Ideally, hyperlinks should be placed within the document as close as possible to their referent. Hyperlinks bunched together at the bottom of the Web page (or worse yet, on a Web page by themselves) do not serve the visiting researcher as well as integrated links. Another problem with hyperlinks is a seemingly endless list of hyperlinks on a single Web page. On poorly conceived pages, the user must scroll through a very long page to find many of the links. A better arrangement for sites with numerous links organizes the links topically, for easy selection by the user. In a hypothetical Web site about dolphins, the author might include links to 30 other Web sites. Rather than list each Web site on a single page, the Web-page author should offer a hyperlink stating "Click here for links to dolphin habitats," "Click here for links to dolphin communication," and so on. By clicking the hyperlink, the user could be taken to another section of the page to see the appropriate hyperlinks.

Appropriate Use of Multimedia

Using modern design programs, Web-page authors can create pages packed with complex graphics, animated text, and sound effects. Many of these effects are attractive and engaging. However, use of complicated graphics and multimedia elements produces two negative by-products: they often distract the user from the information presented and they require time to load onto the user's computer. Thoughtful Web-page designers realize the importance of restraint in Web-page design.

Using the preceding criteria, educators will be able to select Web sites that complement other learning activities in the school. With so many Web sites available, only the best should be considered.

The World Wide Web is an exciting, dynamic environment for the communication of information and ideas. In this chapter, we've only scratched the surface of everything there is to know about it. However, with patience, perseverance, and a love of learning, educators can find the best ways to integrate the resources of the Web into their curricula. Any less denies teachers a valuable teaching tool and their students a wonderful educational resource.

Bibliography

Books

Ann E. Barron and Karen S. Ivers, *The Internet and Instruction: Activities and Ideas* (Englewood, Colo.: Libraries Unlimited Inc., 1996).

Susan E. Feldman and Larry Krumenaker, *The Internet at a Glance* (Medford, N.J.: Information Today, Inc., 1995).

John R. Levine, Carol Baroudi, and Margaret Levine Young, *The Internet for Dummies*, 4th ed. (Foster City, Calif.: IDG Books Worldwide, 1997).

Elizabeth B. Miller, *The Internet Resource Directory for K–12 Teachers and Librarians* (Englewood, Colo.: Libraries Unlimited, Inc., annual).

Internet

Internet Gurus Central Search Page
http://net.gurus.com/search/

WWW FAQ: What are WWW, hypertext and hypermedia?
http://www.boutell.com/faq/htext.htm

Host Distribution by Top-Level Domain Name
http://www.nw.com/zone/WWW/dist-bynum.html

Internet Domain Survey, January 1997 (Produced by Network Wizards)
http://www.nw.com/zone/WWW/report.html

University of Illinois Assigns All Future Commercial Licensing Rights for Mosaic to Spyglass, Inc.
http://www.spyglass.com/newsflash/releases/aug2494_1.html

Netscape Communications Ships Release 1.0 of Netscape Navigator and Netscape Servers
http://home.netscape.com/newsref/pr/newsrelease1.html

Netscape Communications Offers New Network Navigator Free on the Internet
http://home.netscape.com/newsref/pr/newsrelease8.html

University of Illinois and Netscape Communications Reach Agreement
http://home.netscape.com/newsref/pr/newsrelease9.html

A Little History of the World Wide Web (Robert Cailliau)
http://www.w3.org/History.html

1993 Mosaic, an article on Discovery Channel Online
http://www.discovery.com/DCO/doc/1012/world/technology/internetbest/inet1.15.html

1992 Spinning the Web
http://www.discovery.com/DCO/doc/1012/world/technology/internetbest/inet1.14.html

A Short History of Internet Protocols at CERN (Ben Segal)
http://wwwcn.cern.ch/pdp/ns/ben/TCPHIST.html

From the Ether Microsoft and Netscape Open Some New Fronts in the Escalating Web Wars (Bob Metcalfe). Infoworld Publishing Company, Volume 17, Issue 34, August 21, 1995
http://www.infoworld.com/cgi-bin/displayArchives.pl?dt_data34_32.html

History of the Web—WebObjects
http://www.next.com/WebObjects/History.html

Netscape Mark Andreesson: Portal to the Web
Architects of the Web
http://www.architectsoftheweb.com/andresson.html

How was the Web created? Guide to Cyberspace 6.1
http://www.eit.com/web/www.guide/guide.04.html

Tim Berners-Lee: longer bio
http://www.w3.org/People/Berners-Lee/Longer.html

About the World Wide Web
http://www.w3.org/WWW/

Internet in a Box (Technisys Corp.)
http://www.technisys.com/Products/Software/ibox.html

Periodical Articles

James Collins, "High Stakes Winners," *Time* 147, no. 8 (February 19, 1996): 43+.

"How Much Computer for $1000?," *Consumer Reports* 62, no. 8 (August 1997): 6.

Tom Mainelli, "Internet Search Services Show the Way," *PC Novice* 7, no. 10 (October 1996): 77–79.

Tom Mainelli, "Internet 101: A Guide to Understanding 'Net Speak'," *PC Novice* 7, no. 10 (October 1996): 34+.

Alan Phelps, "Browsing for a Web Browser," *PC Novice* 24, no. 10 (October 1996): 26+.

"Q & A," *Smart Computing* 8, no. 5 (May 1997): 96–97.

Valerie Ryan, "Browser Secrets," *PC World* 15, no. 8 (August 1997): 120–34.

"Search and You Shall Find," *PC Novice* 7, no. 10 (October 1996): 79.

Scott Spanbauer, "Bandwidth on Demand," *PC World* 15, no. 8 (August 1997): 158–68.

Joel Strauch, "Internet: The Next Generation," *Smart Computing* 8, no. 6 (June 1997): 83–85.

Joel Strauch, "I Spy a Good ISP," *Smart Computing* 8, no. 5 (May 1997): 71–74.

Joel Strauch, "56K Modems Arrive (Too Soon?)," *Smart Computing* 8, no. 6 (June 1997): 34–36.

Other

Lecture Notes, Technology Training Institute for Library Personnel. Pensacola Junior College, March 1997, Pensacola, Florida. Lecturers: Charlotte M. Sweeney and Bill Waters.

2 The World Wide Web in the School

Schools around the world are exploring the World Wide Web. Some school districts are implementing plans to wire every school under their direction. "Net Days" are being organized as motivation for schools to enter the Web. In the absence of leadership, some educators are paving their own way, using their personal Internet accounts and purchasing a length of telephone extension cord to connect their classroom computers to the World Wide Web. Whether by district plan or teacher ingenuity, the Web has established itself as a fixture in the school.

Because school Internet use is a relatively new concept, many teachers are still deciding the best ways to integrate the resources of the World Wide Web into their current classroom activities. This chapter addresses this issue. First we'll look at four equipment configurations for using the Internet in the classroom. Then we'll address the needs of student Web users. We'll also look at commonly held myths about students and the World Wide Web. As you read, think about the best use of the World Wide Web for your school or classroom. Remember that not every suggestion will work for everyone. The teacher is still the best judge of what will work in his or her classroom.

Classroom Equipment Options

Where does the classroom computer belong? It depends on who you ask. Some educators will say that the computer belongs on the teacher's desk, where it can be used for word processing and grade calculation. Others will claim that it belongs in a learning center, enabling students to drill and practice rote memory skills. These models don't really work for a computer attached to the World Wide Web, do they? Four models for Web-enabled computer use in the classroom are presented in the following sections:

- The Classroom Resource Station
- The Television/Remote Model
- The Video Projector Model
- The SMART Board Model.

Each model serves a different purpose, and the more advanced models require additional purchases. And of course, each model has its own set of advantages and disadvantages.

The Classroom Resource Station

In this model, the computer connected to the World Wide Web serves as a resource for information to complement classroom activities (see fig. 2.1). The computer can access many different Web sites relating to the curriculum. Research for essays and class projects can also be conducted using this resource. Students can follow the many "voyages" taking place on the World Wide Web (for example, Web sites have followed explorers as they bicycle across South America or retrace Amelia Earhart's flight around the world).

Equipment Needed

Using the computer as a resource station requires only the basic equipment configuration described in the first chapter (a good computer system, a modem, and a phone line). Teachers should also consider two additional items: a printer and a 17-inch computer monitor. The printer will allow students to make copies of their findings to take back to their desks or study groups. The larger monitor makes it easier for two or more students to share the screen.

Advantages

The obvious advantage of this simple configuration is the easy access to the World Wide Web. Students working on a variety of topics can find high-quality information at this resource station. Trips to the computer lab or the media center are still available, but not necessary to answer every research question. Several intriguing activities can also be accessed using this setup within a small group format.

Figure 2.1 Classroom resource station.

Disadvantages

The main disadvantage is the small number of students who can use this resource at once. In fact, days may pass before each student gets a turn on the World Wide Web. In this model, the computer is a good resource but probably not a teaching tool. Thirty students huddled around a computer screen is not an effective teaching strategy.

The classroom resource model provides a good first step for World Wide Web integration into the classroom. No investment is needed beyond the basic computer setup. Teachers who recognize and accommodate the model's strengths and shortcomings will acquire a valuable resource for their classroom studies.

The Television/Remote Model

The television/remote model adds an extra dimension to classroom learning. Using this model, the World Wide Web becomes an audiovisual teaching resource as well as a resource station. The video (VGA) output of the

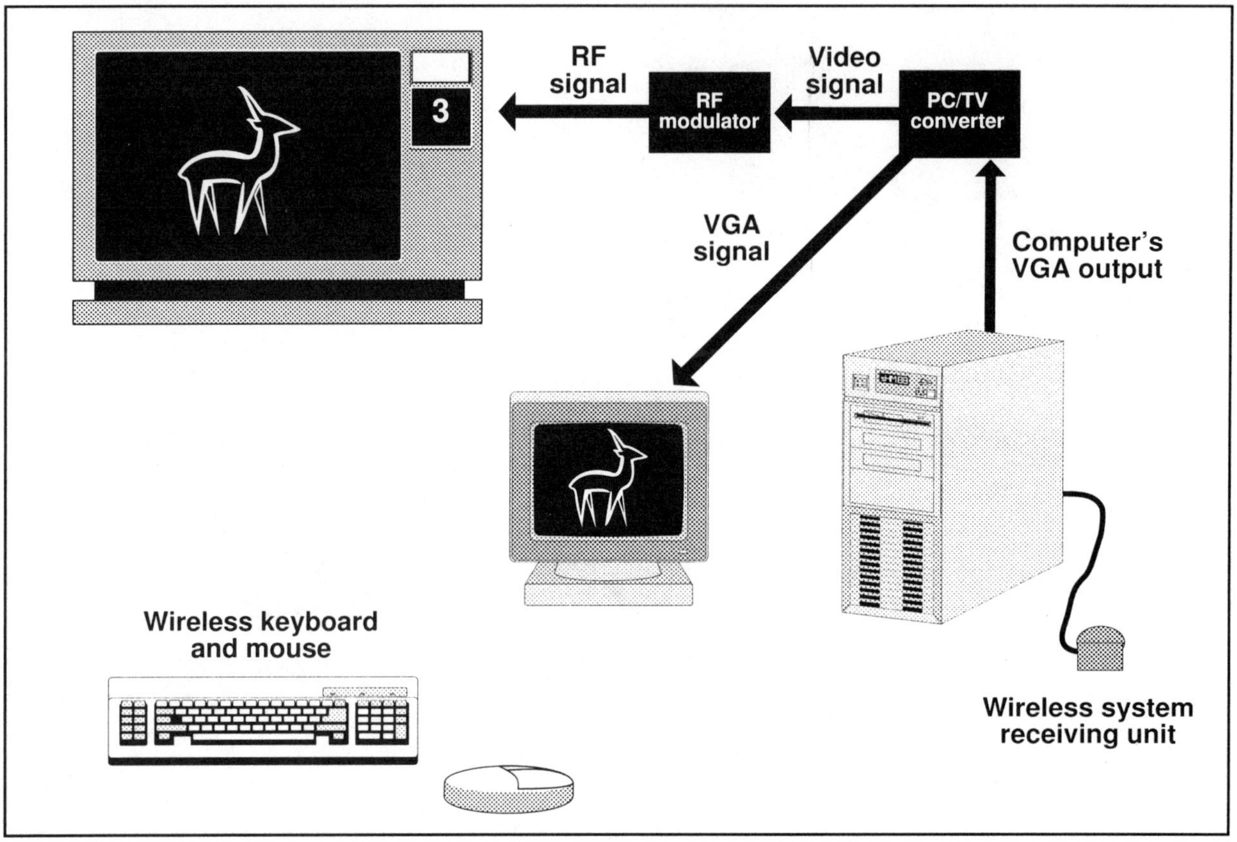

Figure 2.2 Television/remote connection.

computer is connected to a computer/TV signal converter (see fig. 2.2). This converter provides two outputs: the standard VGA signal connected to the computer monitor and a video signal that can be processed by a television/monitor. The information from the World Wide Web appears on both the computer monitor and the classroom television, allowing more students to see the images (see fig. 2.3). This technique is especially effective when graphics-based Web sites (as opposed to text-based Web sites) are used.

Most teachers will want their students to read the text, and standard 12-point type is still tiny on a 27-inch television. The remedy is simple, but seldom explored by educators. By accessing the "options" menu on most Web browsers, the teacher can select a larger font (24-point usually does the trick). All of the text will now appear in this larger font, making the words much easier to read on the television. Many teachers are excited at the prospect of showing Web resources to their students on the classroom television.

This model is further enhanced by the addition of a remote keyboard and a remote mouse (see fig. 2.4). These devices are wireless and work just like a television remote control. A receiving station (about the size of a

Figure 2.3 Television/remote model.

matchbox) is connected to the serial port of the computer. The remote keyboard and mouse (often sold together) send their signals to this receiving station, and the computer treats the wireless devices just like their connected counterparts. The teacher doesn't have to sit at the computer to control it. Teachers and students can use the wireless keyboard and wireless mouse from anywhere in the classroom.

Equipment Needed

A computer as described earlier is needed. A computer with an additional serial port allows easy connection of the wireless receiving station. The wireless keyboard/mouse system is available for purchase through many educational software vendors and costs around $200.

The same vendor can probably provide the computer/TV converter. Basic models sell for about $150; advanced models sell for as much as $500. Make sure that the computer/TV converter you purchase allows for adjustment of the screen size. The basic models don't allow this adjustment, and as a result the screen edges often do not appear on the television screen.

Figure 2.4a A remote keyboard. Photo courtesy of Mind Path Technologies

Figure 2.4b A remote mouse. Photo courtesy of Mind Path Technologies

A 27-inch (diagonal) screen or larger television/monitor is recommended for this model. When selecting a television screen size, apply the 2 × 8 rule (see fig. 2.5). This rule states that no viewer should be closer than two times the screen diagonal, nor farther than eight times the screen diagonal from the television. Using a 27-inch diagonal television, all viewers (students) should be in a zone between 4.5 feet (about 1.5 meters) and 18 feet (about 6 meters) from the screen. Twenty-seven-inch diagonal televisions can be purchased for about $350.

When possible, buy classroom televisions with audio/video input jacks. Remember, the computer/TV converter produces a video signal, not the RF

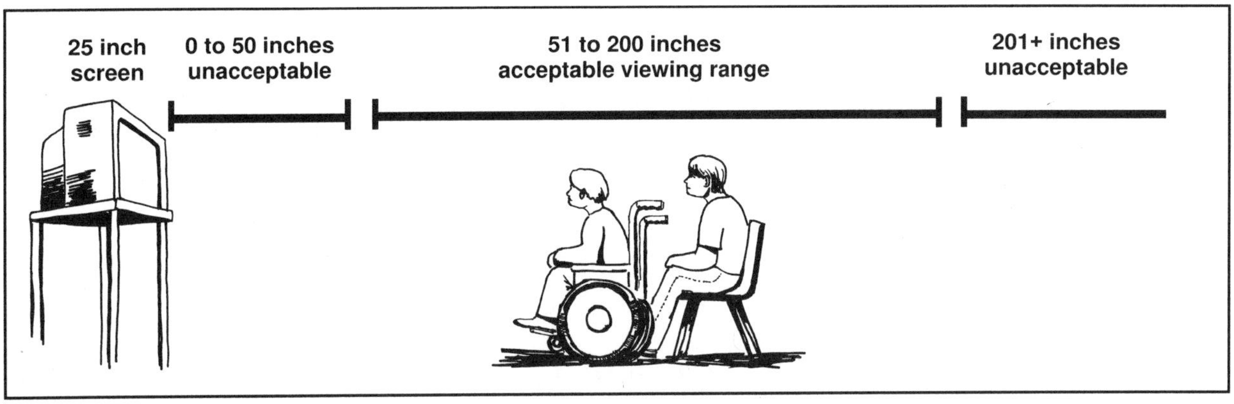

Figure 2.5 The 2 × 8 rule.

signal used by televisions. If you're using a television that doesn't have audio/video inputs, you must modulate the signal. This can be done in two ways. First, a simple RF modulator can be purchased from an electronics dealer. This modulator converts video signal into RF signal. The cost is about $35. The second option is to run the video signal through a VCR, which has its own RF modulator built in. Plug the signal into the video-input jack, usually found on the back of the VCR. Then connect the VCR to the television using the standard RF connection. When the proper input channel is selected on the VCR, the signal from the computer will be displayed on the television.

Advantages

The main advantage of the television/remote model is that the computer can now be used as a teaching and presentation tool as well as a classroom resource. Teachers can select Web sites as part of the lesson-planning process and bookmark those sites for use in the lesson. The large television will allow more students to clearly see the information on the World Wide Web. The remote mouse and keyboard present two distinct advantages: (1) the teacher can operate the computer from anywhere in the classroom, not just behind the computer desk, and (2) students can take turns operating the computer without leaving their seats.

Disadvantages

Extra equipment must be purchased, connected, and operated for this model to be used. The remote keyboard/mouse system requires software installation and some practice. A line of sight between the remote devices and the receiving station must be maintained.

Using lower quality components when creating this system can result in frustration. Lower-end computer/video converters do not offer the screen control and sizing options advised in the preceding section. Televisions with diagonal measurements of less than 27 inches cannot provide adequate viewing in a classroom situation. Viewers may also be disappointed when they view computer information on the television screen; overall picture quality on the television suffers when compared to the typical computer monitor.

Summary

The computer/video converter requires connection and may need software installation as well. Initial setup time for this model for someone with moderate experience in television and computer connections will be about an hour. Educators may need assistance from the media specialist.

The television/remote model makes excellent use of the World Wide Web by incorporating the Web's visual impact into the teaching experience. Educators with patience and some computer experience will find that this model enhances and enriches their classroom instruction.

The Video Projector Model

A video projector is a natural addition to the system described in the preceding section. The computer is connected directly to a video projector (see fig. 2.6) and the image is shown on a projection screen.

Equipment Needed

Of course, an Internet-ready computer is necessary. If possible, the video projector should have an RS-232 connection option. (This is the connector used by computer monitors; see figure 2.7.) A projection screen (which is already in most classrooms) is required, and a media cart is needed for the video projector to rest on.

Advantages

In addition to the advantages listed for previous models, the most obvious advantage to this model is screen size. Displayed images will be large enough for the entire class to see. Modern video projectors are equipped with digital zoom features, which allow screen size to be increased and decreased without moving the projector. Because the video projector uses a computer connection (eliminating the computer/video converter), the projected image will be crisp and clear.

Disadvantages

Video projectors are quite expensive, with prices beginning at about $3,000. Because most schools own only one or two video projectors, this system is

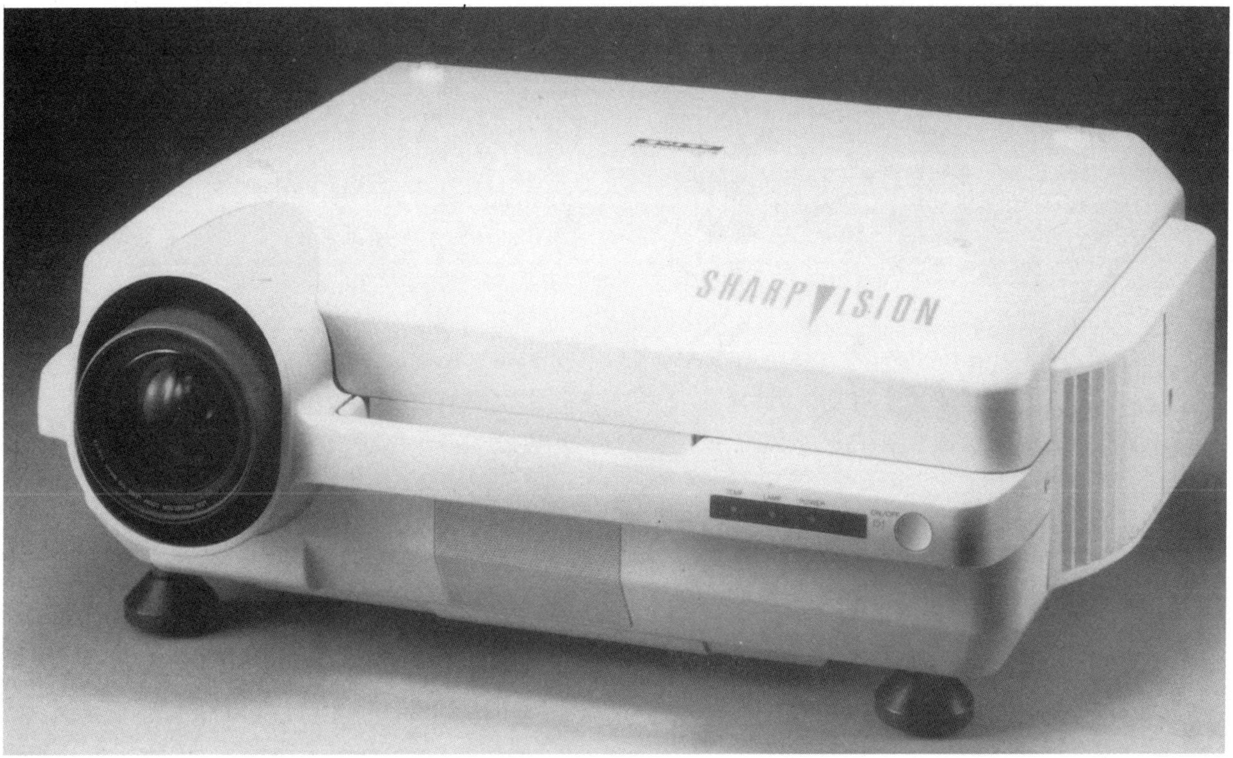

Figure 2.6 Video projector. Photo courtesy of Sharp Electronics Corp.

probably not feasible for each classroom in the school. Video projectors still require a certain amount of experience and patience, although newer models are much more user-friendly than their predecessors. Unless the best (most expensive) model is available, the room will have to be darkened for the projected image to be clear. This darkness may make note-taking and other written work difficult. If an RS-232 computer connection is not available on the video projector, the computer/video converter must still be used, resulting in degradation of picture quality.

Computer placement is also an issue that must be faced in this model. The video projector will probably be placed near the back of the room. Because the computer is connected to the video projector, the computer may have to be relocated to the back of the room as well. An RS-232 extension cable can be purchased, but these cables are expensive and can create a tripping hazard.

Summary

As the power of the presentation progresses, so does the equipment cost and expertise needed to make the experience enriching rather than frustrating.

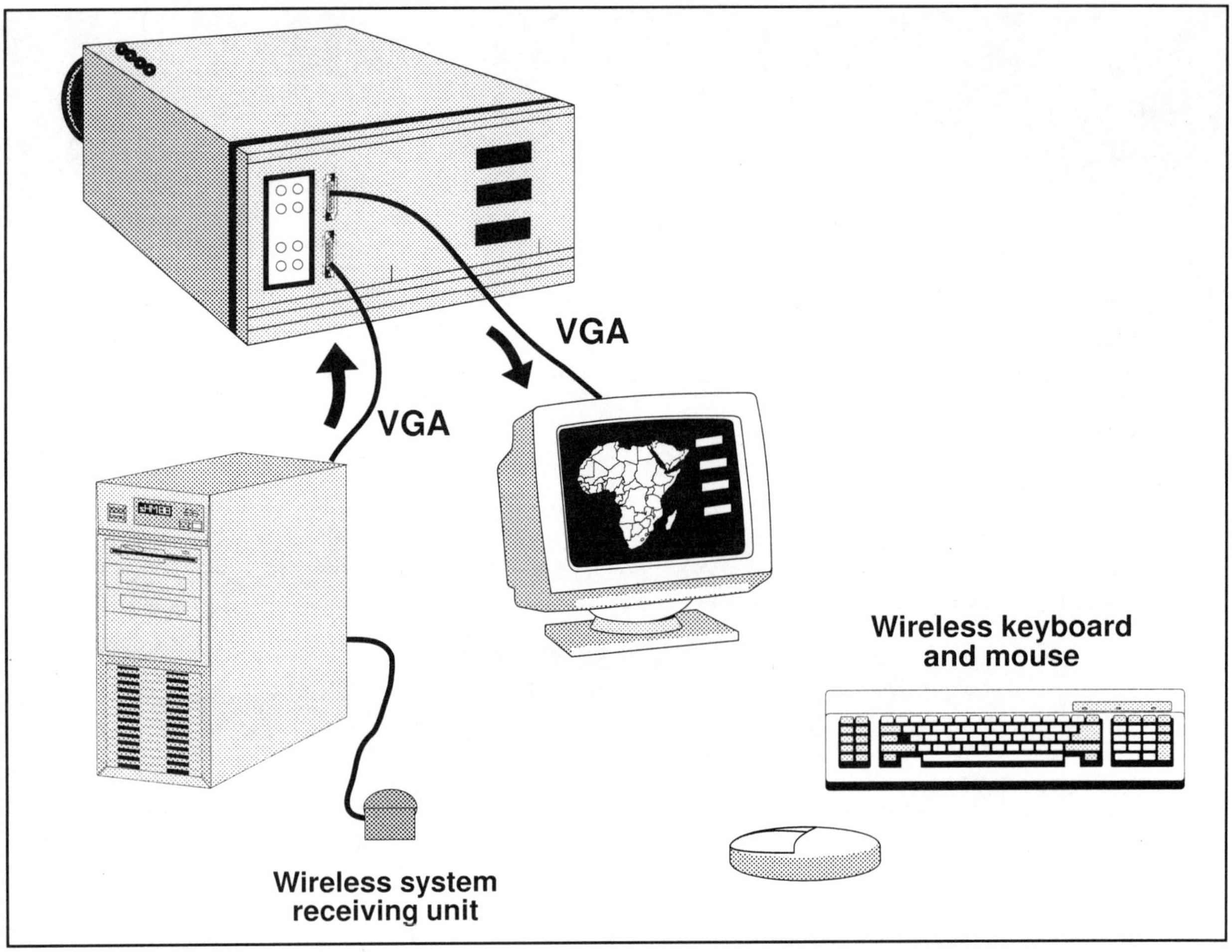

Figure 2.7 Video projector connection.

The video projector model is a great way to present World Wide Web resources to learners. However, educators must master the equipment and schools will need to find funding for equipment purchases.

The SMART Board Model

A new technological development takes the video projector model to the next level. SMART Technologies of Alberta, Canada, markets the SMART Board, a touch-sensitive screen onto which a computer display is projected, using a video projector or overhead projector with LCD panel (see fig. 2.8). When the SMART Board is connected to the computer, it becomes a giant touch-sensitive screen for the video projector (see fig. 2.9). Selecting a World Wide Web hyperlink is as simple as touching its projection on the SMART Board. Special functions allow the user to electronically highlight and make notes on the projection.

Figure 2.8 SMART Board. Photo courtesy of SMART Technologies, Inc.

Advantages

The biggest advantages lie in the freedom given to the teachers and students. Direct interaction with the Web site is possible for anyone who comes to the front of the room.

Disadvantages

Time and money are primary disadvantages. Using a SMART Board is a skill. Educators should plan to spend at least an hour learning the basics of SMART Board operation. Proprietary software must be installed in the computer for SMART Board interaction. The educator should also plan for setup time when the SMART Board and video projector are moved to a new location.

SMART Boards are not inexpensive, with list prices ranging from $1,199 for a 38-inch SMART Board to $2,999 for a 72-inch model. A floor stand costs an extra $300, and shipping may be expensive. Very few schools could afford multiple SMART Boards. The cost of the video projector and the computer must also be considered.

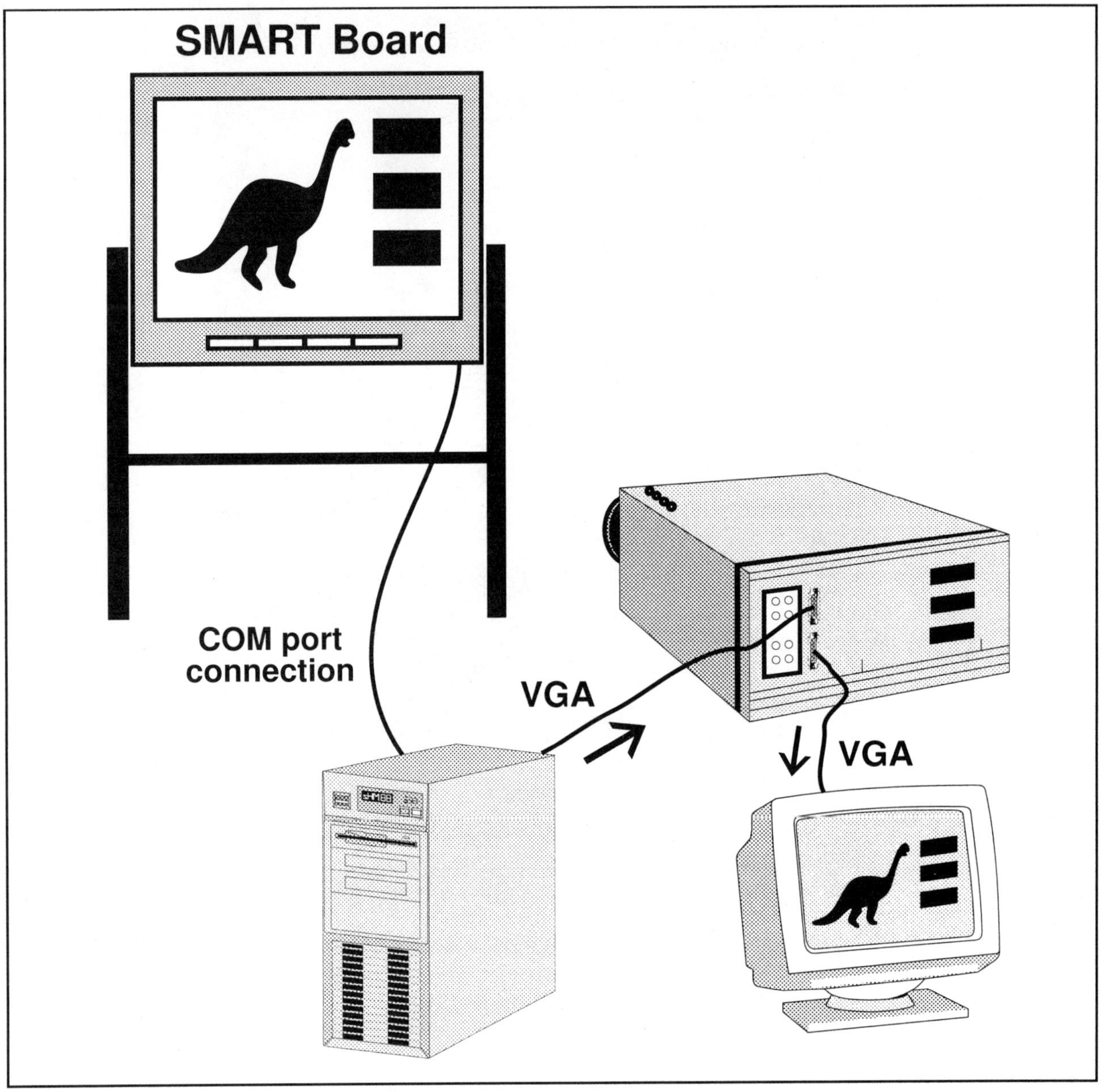

Figure 2.9 SMART Board connection.

Summary

The SMART Board model is the physical manifestation of the hyperlink concept. Just select, and you're there. Realizing the power that its product has in the educational market, and the budget crunches experienced by many schools, the manufacturer has offered discount programs to schools in the past. Contact your local audio/video dealer for information about obtaining a SMART Board at a reduced rate.

The World Wide Web in the School Classroom Equipment Options

	Advantages	Disadvantages
Classroom Resource Station	❑ World Wide Web access ❑ Access to on-line activities (Mayaquest, etc.) ❑ Small investment ❑ Good first step	❑ Limited involvement ❑ Small number of students involved
Television/ Remote Model	❑ Teaching and presentation tool ❑ More student viewing ❑ Teacher no longer tied to computer ❑ Students can operate remote system	❑ Equipment purchase/installation ❑ Lower TV picture quality ❑ Setup time/training
Video Projector Model	❑ Larger screen size ❑ Crisp, clear image	❑ Additional expense ❑ Videoprojector setup time ❑ Darkened room
SMART Board Model	❑ SMART Board direct interaction with World Wide Web	❑ Additional expense ❑ Software installation ❑ SMART Board setup ❑ Learning SMART Board operation

Figure 2.10 System advantages and disadvantages.

Figure 2.10 summarizes and compares the advantages and disadvantages of the various systems.

A Final Note

If your school is just beginning to use the World Wide Web, the more advanced models may seem impractical, unaffordable, and out of reach. Schools with limited access to technology may be overwhelmed by the

Teaching Theater Checklist

- ❑ Internet-ready computer
- ❑ Wireless keyboard/mouse system
- ❑ Video/data projector
- ❑ SMART Board system
- ❑ Amplified speaker system
- ❑ Videodisc player
- ❑ Videocassette recorder (VCR)
- ❑ Visual presentation camera system

Figure 2.11 "Teaching Theater" equipment list.

thought of video projectors and SMART Boards. Surely, a technology plan with a computer, video projector, and SMART Board in every classroom would seem excessive in most school districts. If that's the case with your school, consider designing a "teaching theater" for your school (see fig. 2.11). Purchase a computer system (with wireless keyboard), a video projector, and a SMART Board for your school. Make the system available for teachers to check out and use in their classrooms, just as you would a 16mm projector or a portable CD player. Become an expert, and offer inservice workshops for teachers. Maybe not all of your teachers will be interested in this dynamic presentation technology, but at least a few will take advantage of it.

Students on the World Wide Web

Use of the World Wide Web in a school can take many forms. Internet access is useful in the classroom, the computer lab, and the library media center. Several factors must be considered to optimize World Wide Web use in these diverse areas. In this section, we look at additional issues that must be considered.

Computer Stations and Printers

Computer hardware recommendations were made in chapter 1. Do your best to meet those standards. Students will compare the World Wide Web to CD-ROMs and computer games—they'll expect reasonably quick response to their input. Underpowered computers will lead to slower response times, and students will quickly lose interest.

Be prepared to provide additional service to students using the World Wide Web. Make Web resources part of your library media orientation. This is especially important if most of your students and teachers have little experience in this medium.

Consider a theme for the area in your library media center where students can access the World Wide Web. This will help establish Internet access as an activity different from CD-ROM or school-network searches. A catchy name like "Cyber Central" or "Web Browser" will help students make the distinction (see fig. 2.12). When asked to name the source for their research, many students will answer, "I got it off that computer." Placing the World Wide Web computers in a separate area will remind students that the information was garnered from an off-campus source. This distinction becomes important as students learn to evaluate information based on source credibility and bias.

If you are able to dedicate one or more computers to World Wide Web research, consider using a menu or security program to prohibit other uses. Many well-meaning students will try to impress educators by changing the computer's background colors, adding a screen saver, or resizing the default font. Still others think that computers were made for games, and will try to access any game (even solitaire) on the hard drive. Many security programs on the market prevent these unintended applications.

Students doing research will probably want a hard copy of their findings. Plan to provide access to a printer. Printer sharing devices are available that allow up to four computers to share a single printer. Ink-jet printers are quick, quiet, and inexpensive. If you must charge for printing, try to keep the cost to a minimum and allow free printouts for students who really don't have a nickel to spare.

Figure 2.12 Internet area in a media center.

Providing Web Resources for Students

Direct your students to useful, appropriate web sites. Several resources are available to help you with this task. Subscribe to at least one magazine that recommends web sites. *Yahoo! Internet Life* is quite popular and rarely offensive. About a dozen of these magazines are on newsstand shelves. Purchase a few and subscribe to the magazines that best fit the needs of your students.

Several printed World Wide Web directories are also available in book form. Most notable are:

- *Microsoft Bookshelf Internet Directory* (with CD-ROM for PCs) (Microsoft Press)
- *The Internet Kids Yellow Pages: Special Edition* by Jean Armour Polly (Osborne McGraw-Hill)

- *The Internet Resource Directory for K–12 Teachers and Librarians* by Elizabeth Miller (Libraries Unlimited, annual)

A bookshelf near the World Wide Web computers would be an appropriate place for these books and magazines.

For many years educators have provided lists of recommended books for students. These lists are often called "pathways" or "gateways." Pathways for World Wide Web sites would also be useful. Imagine that a student wants to use the World Wide Web, but doesn't have a specific research question. "What are you interested in?" says the educator. "I like sports," replies the student. Wouldn't a list of 10 favorite sports Web sites be handy? Teachers can make these lists and share them at faculty meetings. These lists can be printed on bookmarks, too. One of the best ways to learn about the Internet is to look up information about hobbies and interests. A pathway to those sites would be very helpful.

Recommend a different Web site to your students each day. Post the URL (**http://www.** etc.) near the World Wide Web computer using a dry-erase board or small bulletin board. "Site of the Day" can be a regular feature in the media center, and provides a great resource for students and teachers who want to learn about the World Wide Web but do not have a research need.

Change your Web browser's home (start-up) page each day. Create a theme for each day (wildlife, sports, etc.) and set your browsers to that page. A click of the mouse button can return the idle computers to an intriguing site.

On the World Wide Web, all 16 million sites are on equal footing. As an educator, you can help students select the most appropriate sites.

Acceptable Use Policies

Many schools, public libraries, and colleges offer World Wide Web access to their students and patrons at little or no cost. These institutions usually require Internet users to sign an acceptable use policy. An *acceptable use policy* (AUP) is a document that describes the rules a user must follow when accessing the Internet. Most school districts, colleges, and public libraries develop acceptable use policies that are usually typed and printed as a document. Users must read and sign the AUP before going online at the institution. Because every school and public library is different, each acceptable use policy is unique. However, most AUPs contain the following elements:

- A brief description of the Internet
- Definitions

- A warning about possible offensive content
- Reasoning behind the institution's decision to provide Internet access
- Intended use of the Internet (some institutions forbid using the Internet for entertainment)
- Forbidden activities (file transfers, uploading, downloading, business use, etc.)
- Statement on e-mail (some institutions provide e-mail accounts, but most do not)
- Penalties and disciplinary actions for policy violations
- Waiver of liability (protects institution from lawsuits)
- Signature/parent signature

An institution's AUP may be as short as one page or as long as several pages, depending on the amount of detail that the authors feel is necessary.

Sample AUPs can be found in several locations. The easiest place to find sample AUPs is on the World Wide Web. Type "acceptable use policy" in a search engine or directory (Alta Vista, Yahoo!) and you'll find many AUPs online. Also, contact school districts and libraries in your area and review their acceptable use policies. Most professionals are happy to share. Then create an AUP for your institution based on the needs of your patrons and your educational/research objectives.

Remember that your AUP, like the World Wide Web itself, is a living document. Don't be afraid to change, add, or delete sections to serve the needs of your patrons, or as new technology becomes available. For example, a local public library with a single Internet connection may have to enforce time limits for patrons on the World Wide Web. However, as the library updates its equipment and communications line, these time limits may be eliminated. An AUP isn't a sacred vow. Just make sure to let all your patrons know when a change in the acceptable use policy is made.

Blocking Objectionable Sites

Although acceptable use policies are designed to lay the ground rules for Internet use, many institutions have decided to block unwanted World Wide Web sites using software specifically designed for that purpose, or by contracting with proxy servers that do the same thing. By using these products or services, the user can make sure that his or her computer does not access certain Web sites or categories of Web sites. Many blocking products are available for retail purchase from software stores and mail-order catalogs. Some products can also be downloaded directly from the Internet.

Blocking Software for Stand-Alone Computers

Installed by the owner onto the computer's hard drive, *blocking software* identifies Web sites accessed by the computer, checks each site against a database, and censors sites that do not meet the software's criteria. Blocking software designed for use by single computers can be found alongside other software products in retail stores and mail-order catalogs. Fewer than a dozen of these products account for most of the sales. At the time of this writing, Cyber Patrol, Cybersitter, Net Nanny, and SurfWatch are the leading blocking products. Each program operates in a slightly different way. Most of the blocking programs include an extensive core list of sites that are automatically blocked. Some programs allow the user to add and delete from this list, using specific URLs (http://www.playboy.com) or keywords ("nudity"). Many of the products offer monthly updates to the core list, usually available by Internet download.

Proxy Servers

Another strategy for blocking World Wide Web sites is the proxy server. As its name indicates, a proxy server takes the place of your regular Internet service provider. For this reason, school district-wide networks that use high-speed communications lines frequently use proxy servers. The user logs on to the proxy server, which acts as an access ramp to the Internet. Objectionable Web sites are blocked by the proxy server and never have the opportunity to appear on the user's screen (see fig. 2.13). A school district Internet supervisor can amend the proxy server's list of blocked sites for one or all users. The proxy server takes the blocking software off of the stand-alone computer and stations it at the network level. By using a proxy server, school districts can be reasonably assured that objectionable Web sites are not being used at schools (or if they are, all the schools are using them!). Typically, the school district pays an access fee to the proxy server based on the number of computers or computer users to be served. Several proxy servers are available; the most common proxy server designed for schools is *Bess*.

Problems with Site-Blocking

Although these products sound like a great investment for schools, their disadvantages are obvious and significant. Consider the size of the World Wide Web; over 16 million Web sites, with a new Web site going online every 30 seconds! Has a computer technician actually visited each Web site before

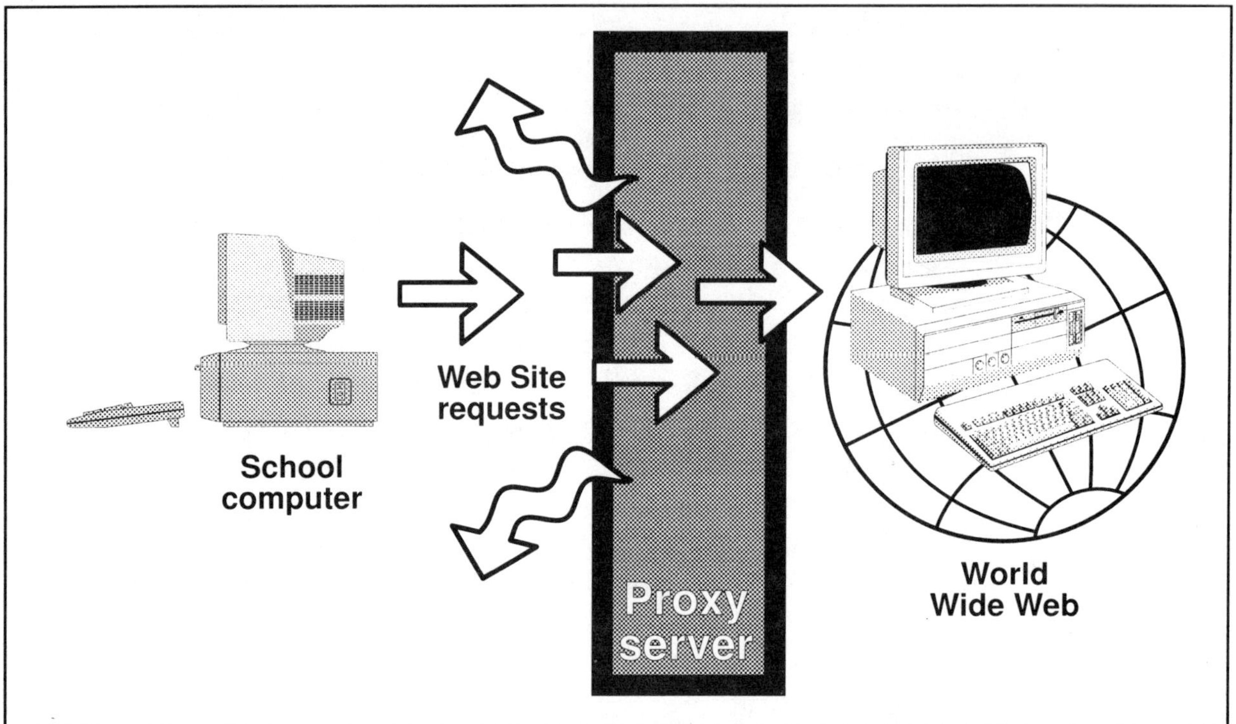

Figure 2.13 Proxy server connection.

adding it to the core list? Probably not. Instead, most of these programs look for keywords, which may or may not reflect objectionable material. Blocking software that eliminates all Web sites with the word "breast" blocks out not only nudity, but also breast cancer studies and most chicken recipes, too! Most proxy servers attempt to visit each Web site; they hire several staffers to do just that. However, the task still appears to be monumental.

Another problem involves the technical expertise required to customize the products. One blocking product blocks only a few hundred Web sites automatically; the user must block the rest. And—let's face it—most adults can't even program a VCR! If a parent or teacher can program it, a precocious student can probably find a way to subvert the block. Proxy servers present less of a problem, because the blocking software is not on the user's computer but on the server itself.

The potential for politically based blocking also exists. What if a blocking software product blocked all non-Christian religious Web sites? Or all pro-life Web sites? Or all Web sites about hunting or fishing? The age-old question, "Who watches the watchmen?" takes on new meaning when blocking Web sites.

Finally, it should be noted that the American Library Association objects to the use of such products. "Access to Electronic Information,

Services, and Networks: An Interpretation of the Library Bill of Rights" was adopted by the ALA Council in 1996. It addresses several issues concerning library Internet access, and should be reviewed by any educational body offering Internet access to its students and faculty.

Ultimately, the decision to electronically block objectionable web sites must be made locally, as close to the user level as possible. Most blocking software is fraught with flaws, loopholes, and inconsistencies. However, the interest in these products is prevalent, as parents and educators seek to protect children from the hazards of the World Wide Web.

The Real Answer: Supervising Students

After reading the previous section and observing all the hullabaloo about blocking objectionable web sites, you may be wondering why anyone would want to bring the World Wide Web into schools in the first place. This reaction is quite natural. But don't let the few "bad apples" of the Internet spoil the barrel. Through thoughtful adult supervision, students can be steered away from objectionable web sites and directed to the thousands of useful sites available.

The flag of freedom is important. I have defended challenged literature in front of the local school board on more than one occasion. However, that flag cannot blind us to a major tenet of the educational system: supervision. When a student or patron enters the media center, does the media specialist ignore him or her? Certainly not! A good media specialist greets the visitor and asks what services he or she requires. Even if the student is coming to enjoy leisure-reading material, the media specialist is still close by. Should this supervisory role be abandoned just because a student decides to use the Internet? No. Ask students about their interests and help them find web sites that meet their needs. Use the books, magazines, and search engines described in this book to help students find appropriate web sites.

Accessing inappropriate web sites should be dealt with using the same criteria that you would use if the material were in another medium. For example, suppose a student purposely accesses a pornographic web site. Consider the school policy if the same student pulled a pornographic magazine from his or her book bag and began to read it in the media center. What would you do (after you regained consciousness)? You would probably confiscate the material. You might even consult a school administrator or make a phone call to the parent. The World Wide Web deserves no preferential treatment. Just like books, magazines, and videos, the World Wide Web is a medium for communicating ideas. Don't ignore professional standards in the name of technology.

In closing, consider this true story experienced by the author during his first year of providing World Wide Web access to students. A seventh-grader asked if he could access a Web site that he had seen in a television commercial. This was fine with me. He sat at the computer keyboard, and typed **http://www.bolla.com**. A few seconds later, the Bolla Wine home page appeared on the screen. He grinned sheepishly. I examined his expression and was instantly convinced that he was not a 12-year-old wino. I didn't have to ask him what he had expected to find on the Web site; his expression told me that he was more surprised than I was.

What was my response? Did I yell and scream? Did I suspend his Internet privileges? No. I simply said, "Can you think of anything you'd like to look up on the Internet?"

"Basketball!" he quickly gasped.

"Let's try NBA.com," I said. He typed in the URL, and in a few seconds he was blissfully reading basketball scores and researching the statistics of his favorite players.

Did he really want to look up wine on the World Wide Web? Of course not. He just wanted to use the Internet because he'd heard so much about it. All he needed was someone to point him in the right direction.

So, you have students who really want to look up wine on the Web? That's another book, my friends.

Myths About Students and the World Wide Web

The World Wide Web presents a significant opportunity for teachers and students. The organization of computer data for easy access by anyone with a computer, a phone line, and an Internet account is truly the most important communications event of this generation. However, like most revolutionary developments, the World Wide Web has been oversold, its applications and possibilities overstated. Here are a few myths that you may have heard about the World Wide Web, and its place in education, followed by the logic supporting a more reasonable attitude to this tremendous resource.

Myth: Everything on the World Wide Web is fun!

Many educators and students are disappointed when they discover that the World Wide Web isn't entertaining in the ways that we have come to expect from TV, radio, and motion pictures. Sure, there's a lot of great information on the Internet, and most of it is presented in an eye-catching way. But fun is an overstatement. This "fun" perception is probably due to Web site sponsors promoting their Web sites as entertainment media. Because I am a stock car racing fan, one of my favorite Web sites is NASCAR Online (**http://www.nascar.com**). This excellent site features photos of every driver, every car, complete race results—just about everything you'd want to know about NASCAR. But visiting the Web site is not nearly as much fun as visiting a racetrack, watching a race on television, or talking with friends about racing. NASCAR Online also features audio and video clips for downloading, but the downloading process takes several minutes, and I can get much better audio and video from any of the several television and radio shows about stock car racing. Most professional Web sites are very informative and pleasing to the eye, but "fun" is an overstatement using most people's definition of entertainment.

Myth: All kids will be excited by the Internet.

Computer and software salespeople state this myth frequently, but my experience says it just isn't so. Many students aren't terribly interested in the medium, and feel much better collecting research facts from print sources. Certainly, students should learn how to navigate the Web if their plans include a higher education. Just don't expect everyone to be enthralled by the Web.

Myth: The World Wide Web is easier to use than print.

In most cases research on the World Wide Web presents more challenges than using print counterparts. Internet users must not only search for Web sites that fit their topic, they must also weed out useless Web sites and be wary of incorrect information. Most students find reading from a computer screen tiring, and the World Wide Web offers many distractions for younger students. Using the World Wide Web is an acquired skill that in many ways is more difficult than print research.

Myth: The World Wide Web will eventually replace print sources (and its brother: *We don't have to buy so many books, because we've got the Internet*).

Until Internet service providers can come up with a way to pay creators for their intellectual property, print materials will be with us. Book, magazine, and software publishing is a large industry. Payment for writing and production is an important motivator for authors (trust me). Unfortunately, some uninformed educators and administrators see all of the information available on the World Wide Web and assume that library book and software budgets can be slashed. *This is not true.* The World Wide Web doesn't replace many books in our collections. It simply gives us access to materials that we could not otherwise afford or are not available in print. No one wants to crawl under the covers and read a computer screen. The World Wide Web can't be read on a school bus, in a subway, or on the beach. Printed materials and their educational software counterparts will always be an important part of the literacy experience.

Myth: The World Wide Web links students to the whole world.

Not true. Sure, the World Wide Web gives us access to information that we might not otherwise have had. We can also e-mail people in countries across the globe. But many people do not have access to the Internet and will probably never have Internet access. The World Wide Web is virtually unknown by huge sections of the global population.

In a 1997 article, *Parade* magazine reported that of the 5.6 billion people in the world, 4.7 billion live in the Third World. That means that 84 percent of the world population probably doesn't have access to a telephone, much less a computer and an Internet service provider. More than half the world's population lives on less than $2 a day. World Wide Web access is probably not a high priority for these people. China's population is about 1.2 billion, but there are fewer than 20,000 Web page domains in China. India, which has almost a billion residents, has about 3,000 domains, behind much smaller countries like Latvia, Finland, and Estonia. And do governments that repress human rights want their citizens to have World Wide Web access? Probably not. We all know the effect that a free press has on repressed citizens.

That's not to say that the World Wide Web isn't growing, or that more people won't eventually join this cyber-community. But "world wide" refers to the potential of the Web, not the current saturation.

Myth: The World Wide Web is the great equalizer.

This is more a myth of semantics than of representation. I believe this phrase originally referred to the ability of persons with varying disabilities and physical challenges to share ideas over the World Wide Web without encountering the boundaries that many challenged individuals face each day. On the Web, everyone is equal. A by-product of this equalizing power places offending web sites in the same category as useful sites. A racist organization is just as easy to find as the Library of Congress on the World Wide Web. This type of equality we don't need.

The Web may have an equalizing effect on communications, but don't tell that to people who don't have Internet access. At my school, about half of the students surveyed reported having no World Wide Web access at home. As the ability to access web sites becomes more important in the educational process, we are in danger of creating a group of technological have-nots. This makes a strong case for student Internet access in schools and public libraries.

Myth: Kids know more about the Internet than adults do.

Most educators can name at least one child who is a true Internet whiz. They're plugged-in, logged-on, and in-tune to everything Internet. That's the myth. The reality is that even though they have some experience on the superficial level, they probably don't know how to apply the World Wide Web to the educational setting.

One of my former students fit this mold. He spent at least a couple of hours every night on America Online and even had his own home page. But his time online was spent mostly on chat-room conversation and downloading demonstration copies of video games. He didn't know how to use a search engine, how to save a file, or how to type a URL. When I discovered this, I took a few minutes to show him these strategies. As you can guess, he quickly learned the process, and is now an excellent World Wide Web user.

How many of these students do we have in each class? One or two? Remember that most of your students need to learn the World Wide Web from the ground floor. Don't be intimidated by the one or two experienced students.

You can probably think of your own myths to add to the list. Remember the old adage: anything that sounds too good to be true probably is. The World Wide Web provides so many great opportunities for educators that there's no need to oversell it. An informed educator can think of several uses for this wonderful resource. Most teachers don't need to be rescued from the classroom—they just need a little help every now and then.

Perhaps your school's commitment to the World Wide Web is a single computer station in the media center. Or maybe you have a T-1 line that gives lightning-fast Internet access to every classroom. Just remember that teaching and learning are still the foundation of all education. No technology can replace that. Don't abdicate your classroom to a computer and a roll of copper wire. Work *with* your students as they learn about this wonderful educational resource.

The World Wide Web isn't the end of teaching. It's just a new beginning.

Bibliography

Books

John R. Levine, Carol Baroudi, and Margaret Levine Young, *The Internet for Dummies,* 4th ed. (Foster City, Calif.: IDG Books Worldwide, 1997).

Elizabeth B. Miller, *The Internet Resource Directory for K–12 Teachers and Librarians* (Englewood, Colo.: Libraries Unlimited Inc., annual).

Internet

Access to Electronic Information, Services and Networks: An Interpretation of the LIBRARY BILL OF RIGHTS (American Library Association)
Gopher://ala.ala.org:70/00/alagophx/alagophxfreedom/e/ecctacc.fin

What You Need to Know About Acceptable Use Policies (CoVis Network)
http://www.covis.nwu.edu/AUP-archive/CoVis_AUP.html

Okaloosa County Acceptable Use Policy—Adopted 8-12-97
Wysiwyg://15/http://www.fuw.gulf.net/~kanel/aypolicy/aupolicy.htm

School District of Okaloosa County Parent or Guardian Internet Responsibility Contract
http://www.okaloosa.k12.fl.us/techcom/mis5251.htm

Internet Gurus Central Search Page
http://net.gurus.com/search/

Host Distribution by Top-Level Domain Name
http://www.nw.com/zone/WWW/dist-bynum.html

Internet Domain Survey, January 1997 (produced by Network Wizards)
http://www.nw.com/zone/WWW/report.html

Periodical Articles

"Acceptable Use Policies: Defining What's Allowed Online and What's Not," *Classroom Connect* (December 1994/January 1995).

Jane Ciabattari, "The World's Have-Nots" (Parade's Special Intelligence Report), *Parade, The Sunday Newspaper Magazine*, August 17, 1997, page 15.

"How Much Computer for $1000?," *Consumer Reports* 62, no. 8 (August 1997): 6.

"Shielding Your Kids," *Consumer Reports* 62, no. 5 (May 1997): 30.

Other

Lecture Notes, Technology Training Institute for Library Personnel, Pensacola Junior College, March 1997, Pensacola, Florida. Lecturers: Charlotte M. Sweeney and Bill Waters.

Teacher Plans and Activity Sheets

Teacher Plan

Bartlett, John. 1901. Familiar Quotations

Before the Internet exercise

1. Lead a class discussion on the following questions: Why do people value quotations? Why would someone create a book of quotations?
2. Ask the students about quotes that they have heard. Be ready to stimulate responses with quotations, such as:

   "Ask not what your country can do for you—ask what you can do for your country."—*John F. Kennedy*

   "I have been to the mountaintop. I have seen the promised land."—*Martin Luther King, Jr.*

   "That's one small step for [a] man; one giant leap for mankind."—*Neil Armstrong*
3. Ask students why and when they might need to use a quotation. List their ideas on the board.

After the Internet exercise

1. Make a class quote guide. Students can use a desktop publishing program to create a booklet of their favorite quotes.
2. Formulate a class list of modern slogans and sayings that students hear in the news, in political campaigns, and in the media. Have the class decide if these have enough "staying power" to survive as quotations for future generations.
3. Lead an investigation into Project Bartleby using the resources on the home page described in the Super Surfer question.
4. With your class, investigate copyright as it applies to Project Bartleby. Lead a class discussion on the following topic: Will all books be on the World Wide Web one day? Why or why not?
5. Present the class with modern quotation guides found in your school or local public library. Have students compare these guides to the quotes on this Web page.

Bartlett, John. 1901. Familiar Quotations

http://www.columbia.edu/acis/bartleby/bartlett

1. Locate a quotation for each of the following topics. Try to select a quotation that tells us something about the author's insight into the subject area. Make sure to note the author of each quote.

Freedom	Courage	Morality
Honesty	Government	Wealth
Love	Humor	Friendship

2. What quotation does John Bartlett write in the "Front Matter" to begin his quotation book?
3. What is the first copyright date given for *Familiar Quotations*?
4. List a few instances when you might need to use *Familiar Quotations* or another quote guide.

Super Surfer

Use the link to go to the "Project Bartleby" home page. What appears to be the goal of this project? Give examples to support your answer.

Kowabunga Dude!

Make a collection of at least 10 quotations that reflect the opinions of your friends, your teacher, and your parents. You may also want to list quotations found in the media, like "Just do it!" Organize the quotes into a mini-quote book of your own.

Teacher Plan

The Complete Works of William Shakespeare

Before the Internet exercise

1. Ask the students to make a list of what they know about William Shakespeare. Combine the facts on the board. Be prepared to correct inaccuracies.
2. Talk to students about Shakespearean plots. Ask them to compare the story lines to movies they have seen.
3. Assign reports on the time period in which Shakespeare lived. Topics could include British government, family life, religion, warfare, and so on.

After the Internet exercise

1. Ask students if they have ever heard any of the quotations in the exercise. Lead a discussion about the meaning of the quotes.
2. Lead a discussion about the types of plays Shakespeare might write if he were alive today.
3. Find an age-appropriate video of a Shakespearean play. Show a portion to the class.

The Complete Works of William Shakespeare

http://the-tech.mit.edu/Shakespeare/works.html

1. Use the "Search" function on this Web site to find the name of the play in which these famous lines appear.

   "Full fathom five thy father lies; Of his bones are coral made"

   "He that hath a beard is more than a youth, and he that hath no beard is less than a man."

   "The devil can cite Scripture for his purpose"

   "What's in a name? That which we call a rose by any other name would smell as sweet."

   "A horse! A horse! My kingdom for a horse!"

   "Cowards die many times before their deaths; The valiant never taste of death but once."

   "We cannot all be masters, nor all masters cannot be truly follow'd."

2. Name the three groups in which Shakespeare's plays are classified. When did this practice of arrangement begin? Was it during Shakespeare's lifetime?
3. In addition to plays, what other type of literature did Shakespeare write?
4. According to the Chronological Listing of Plays, which play was written first? When was it written?
5. Which was the last play to be written by Shakespeare? When was it written? What unusual tragedy occurred during an early performance of this play?

Super Surfer

Go to one of the sites listed in the section "Shakespeare Resources on the Internet." Spend a few minutes at that site. Write a paragraph about your findings, and share it with the class.

Kowabunga Dude!

Go the Web site "Shakespeare and the Globe" at **http://www.rdg.ac.uk/globe/Data-Base/Images/NewGlobe.html**. Write a brief report on the new Globe Theatre.

Teacher Plan

The Page at Pooh Corner

Before the Internet exercise

1. Lead a class discussion in which students tell everything they know about Winnie the Pooh and the characters in the Pooh stories. (They may not be aware of the original Pooh books and verse.)
2. Read excerpts from some of the original Pooh books to the class. Then show a videotaped portion of the modern cartoon "The New Adventures of Winnie the Pooh." Lead students in a compare/contrast discussion.
3. Ask students about other fictional characters that have been used in entertainment by the media (the Walt Disney company is especially active in this area). Ask students their opinions about the practice of retelling classic stories and myths. What responsibilities rest with the movie producers?

After the Internet exercise

1. Lead a class discussion about what students have learned from this exercise.
2. Assign readings from the original Winnie the Pooh books. Have students prepare oral readings.
3. Have students illustrate their favorite scenes from the Pooh stories.

The Page at Pooh Corner

http://chaos.trxinc.com/jmilne/Pooh

1. Who wrote the books *Winnie-the-Pooh* and *The House at Pooh Corner*? Who was the illustrator for these books?
2. In what decade were the books first published?
3. What was Winnie-the-Pooh's real name in the first books?
4. How many different language translations are available for *Winnie-the-Pooh*?
5. When was A. A. Milne born?
6. What was the name of A. A. Milne's only son (born in 1920)? What important gift did that son receive on his first birthday?
7. What real-life place inspired the setting for the Winnie-the-Pooh books? What large city is it near?
8. Which Winnie-the-Pooh characters were based on stuffed animals in the Milne nursery? Where are the original stuffed animals displayed?
9. What kind of bear was the real-life Winnie? Who was the bear's original owner?
10. Which recording artist wrote a song about Winnie-the-Pooh in 1969?

Super Surfer

Use the "links" page to visit another Winnie-the-Pooh Web site. Compare that site with this one.

Kowabunga Dude!

Why do you think Winnie-the-Pooh continues to be such a popular character? Ask your friends for their answers and share the results with the class.

Teacher Plan

National Earthquake Information Center

Before the Internet exercise

1. Conduct a class discussion about earthquakes. Find out what your students know about earthquakes. Can they name any famous earthquakes, or parts of the world where earthquakes are most likely to occur? What causes earthquakes?
2. Discuss the National Earthquake Information Center. Why might such a facility be important? What tasks would your students give an earthquake center?
3. Ask students to estimate the number of earthquakes that occur each year and the damage caused by earthquakes.

After the Internet exercise

1. Use an encyclopedia, science book, atlas, or almanac to compare earthquakes with other natural disasters. Is one type of disaster better or worse to experience than any other? Why or why not?
2. Investigate building structural codes as they relate to earthquakes. Invite an architect or engineer to speak about how earthquakes relate to building design and construction. Do other countries have similar standards?
3. Collect magazine articles, newspaper clippings, and Internet news about earthquakes. Make a bulletin board as a class project.

National Earthquake Information Center

http://wwwneic.cr.usgs.gov

1. Where is the National Earthquake Information Center located?
2. On this Web site, find the location of three recent earthquakes. For each earthquake that you select, list the date, the location, and the damage that it caused (deaths, injuries, and structures).
3. How many "Significant Earthquakes of the World" are listed for the most recent year? Is this number more or less than you expected?
4. Load the "Current Earthquake Map" for your area of the world. Which earthquake is closest to where you live?
5. Which states in the United States have the most earthquakes? Which states have the fewest earthquakes?
6. How long can an earthquake shake?
7. How many "major" and "great" earthquakes occur on the average each year? How many minor earthquakes occur every year?
8. What was the location of the most destructive earthquake on record? When did it occur?
9. When and where did the largest earthquake in the United States occur?

Super Surfer

Go to the "Geologic Hazards" page of this Web site. Select one of the categories presented. Visit at least three of the recommended web-sites and prepare a brief report on your findings. Present your report to the class.

Kowabunga Dude!

Using information found on this Web site or in another reference source, make a model illustrating plate tectonics. Show the class how the continents have moved over the last 200 million years.

Teacher Plan

Volcano World

Before the Internet exercise

1. Conduct a class discussion to discover what students know about volcanoes. Make a list of the facts on the board. Have any of your students ever seen a volcano? If so, when and where?
2. Locate several Pacific Ocean islands on a map. Ask students to hypothesize how volcanic activity played a part in the formation of these islands.
3. Use a map to identify places of recent volcanic eruptions. Ask students to trace a pattern of volcanic activity.

After the Internet exercise

1. On a map or globe, mark the volcanic activity that students found on this Web site.
2. Share the Kowabunga Dude! activities with the class. Make a videotaped program featuring a "Live—On the Scene" report of the volcanic activity. Ask the reporter to describe what he or she is seeing as the volcano model erupts.
3. Ask students to depict a volcanic eruption in artwork and poetry. Display their work on a class bulletin board.

Volcano World

http://volcano.und.nodak.edu/

1. Where is the last updated volcano activity?
2. When did that volcano begin erupting?
3. What is the current status of this volcano?
4. Select five volcanoes from the active volcano list. For each volcano that you list, note where the volcano is located, when it began erupting, and its current status.
5. Which active volcano is closest to where you live? Have you heard about it before?
6. What happened today in volcano history? (If today is not a "volcano history" day, use the closest day listed.)

From the "Ask a Volcanologist" questions:

1. What is the difference between magma and lava?
2. How hot is lava?
3. How does a volcano affect the weather?
4. What are three good things that volcanoes do?

Super Surfer

Go to the "Volcanic Parks and Monuments" section. Select one of the parks listed and plan a trip to the park. Include different activities that you could do in the park, how you would get there, and so on.

Kowabunga Dude!

Make a working model of a volcano. Be safe—no fire allowed! Use the book *Janice VanCleave's Volcanoes* (John Wiley & Sons).

Teacher Plan

The Heart: An On-Line Exploration

Before the Internet exercise

1. Obtain a model of the human heart from the science or biology lab. Have students examine the model and hypothesize about the functions of each section.
2. Discuss the word *heart* and all that it means in the English language. With what character traits is the heart associated? What does it mean to say, "That team really has heart!"? Why do you think these associations have been made?
3. Using an encyclopedia (print or electronic), almanac, or other reference books as resources, lead a class discussion on the importance of keeping your heart healthy.

After the Internet exercise

1. Invite a local surgeon or doctor to speak about the heart. Ask him or her to bring simple instruments used to evaluate heart health.
2. Ask the physical education teacher or school nurse to talk to the class about exercises designed to keep the heart healthy. Lead the class in a brief exercise session.
3. Visit the Web site of the American Heart Association (**http://www.amhrt.org**). Read about the steps they are taking in the area of heart health.
4. Ask students to draw pictures of activities that promote a healthy heart. Post the drawings on a "Healthy Heart" bulletin board.
5. Sponsor a slogan contest about heart health.

The Heart: An On-Line Exploration

http://sln2.fi.edu/biosci/heart.html

1. How many times does the human heart beat in an average lifetime?
2. What are the average heart rates for:
   a. An infant?
   b. A 7-year-old?
   c. An 18-year-old?
3. How many cavities make up the heart? What are their names?
4. What is another name for the main artery of the heart?
5. What is the name of the vessel that connects the heart with the lungs?
6. How much blood is inside the body of an average adult?
7. What are the four types of blood? Which type is considered the "universal donor"?
8. What is the name of the instrument that a health care professional uses to listen to your heart?
9. What is a heart murmur?
10. According to this page, what two factors led to an increase in heart disease?
11. What surgeon performed the first whole-heart transplant? What year did it take place?
12. Which doctor implanted the first permanent artificial heart? Who designed that heart?

Super Surfer

Find the three steps included in "Healthy Heart—A Prescription for Living." Write a two-sentence description for each of these steps.

Kowabunga Dude!

Complete the heartbeat activity described at activity link (**http://sln2.fi.edu/biosci/activity/bio-2.html**). Make sure to work with your teacher on this activity.

Teacher Plan

The Faces of Science: African Americans in the Sciences

Before the Internet exercise

1. Discuss and list all of the different areas that are considered "science." List career possibilities in the sciences.
2. Discuss obstacles encountered by African Americans in previous generations who wanted to pursue college degrees.
3. Identify African American community leaders. Ask one of the leaders to visit your class and speak about opportunities and obstacles.

After the Internet exercise

1. Ask students to create a picture of one of the scientists mentioned on the Web site. Create a bulletin board.
2. Research the United Negro College Fund (**http://www.uncf.org**). How has this organization helped African Americans gain access to education?
3. Read excerpts from Booker T. Washington's *Up from Slavery* to the class.

The Faces of Science: African Americans in the Sciences

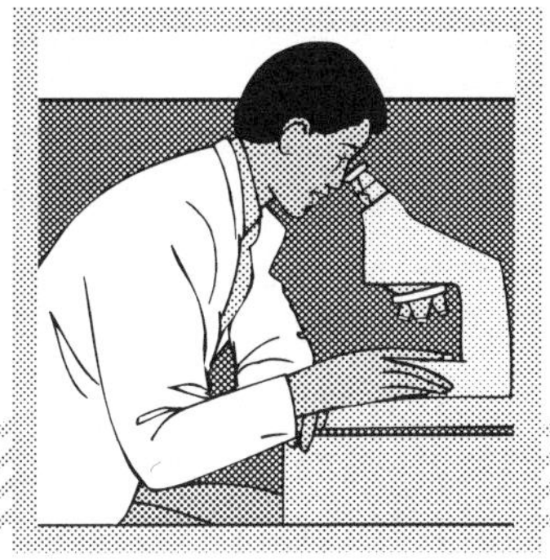

http://www.lib.lsu.edu/lib/chem/display/faces.html

1. What was the specialty of biochemist Samuel Lee Kountz, Jr.?
2. Biologist Roger Arliner Young was the first black woman to ___________.
3. What did chemist George Washington Carver, Jr. call his work with agricultural products?
4. Name five of the synthetic products developed by Dr. Carver.
5. In what field does physicist Katherine G. Johnson apply her knowledge of physics and mathematics?
6. Name five projects developed by engineer Archibald Alexander and his construction firm.
7. Name three of Frederick M. Jones's inventions.
8. What types of problems does computer scientist Annie Easly tackle?
9. In what famous Army Air Force regiment did meteorologist Charles Edward Anderson serve?
10. Charles Drew was an accomplished physician and surgeon. What common hospital division did Dr. Drew originate?
11. What famous first surgery did Dr. Daniel Hale Williams perform?
12. What type of animal was zoologist Charles Henry Turner's specialty?

Super Surfer

Selecting oceanographer Evan B. Forde's name will take you to his personal Web page. Forde works for the NOAA. What do the letters NOAA stand for? What is the main mission of the NOAA?

Kowabunga Dude!

Investigate science education opportunities by visiting the Web site of a college or university in your state. Send e-mail requesting a brochure.

Teacher Plan

The Weather Channel

Before the Internet exercise

1. Discuss the importance of weather information. Where do students get their weather information? In which career fields is weather information important?
2. Ask students to imagine life before accurate weather forecasting.
3. Assign brief reports on the tools used to forecast the weather. Have students share their reports with the class.

After the Internet exercise

1. Present a two-minute television weather forecast as a class assignment. In groups, have students research the weather information and decide which facts to include. The weather reporters can be videotaped in front of a map.
2. Ask a local weather forecaster or television weather anchor to speak to the class.
3. Find a copy of *The Old Farmer's Almanac*. Compare the book's weather predictions with the Weather Channel's forecast and the actual weather for several days. Which is more accurate?
4. Investigate meteorological societies and organizations:

   The American Meteorological Society—**http://www.ametsoc.org/AMS/**

   The International Society of Biometeorology—**http://www.es.mq.edu.au/ISB/**

   The National Weather Association—**http://www.nwas.org**

   The World Meteorological Association—**http://www.wmo.ch**

   Why do they exist? What are their objectives?

The Weather Channel

http://www.weather.com

1. Select your state on the weather channel main page. Find the city nearest your location on the selection screen. List the current conditions and the forecast (high temperature, low temperature, and precipitation) for the next three days.
2. View the regional Doppler radar for your area. Describe (in your own words) the likelihood of rain or snow coming your way.
3. Load the satellite photo of your area. How does it compare to the Doppler radar? What things are the same and what things are different?
4. Find tomorrow's weather forecast (high temperature, low temperature, precipitation) for the following international cities:

   Lagos, Nigeria — Melbourne, Australia
   San Jose, Costa Rica — Beirut, Lebanon
   Karachi, Pakistan — Manila, Philippines
   Helsinki, Finland — Ocho Rios, Jamaica

Super Surfer

Go to the "Health and Allergies" page on this Web site. Look at several of the allergy maps available. Describe your area's exposure to allergens in the next few days.

Kowabunga Dude!

1. Using your area's five-day weather forecast, draw a picture depicting what you think the satellite photograph will look like. Compare your results to the actual satellite photograph when it becomes available.
2. Write down the five-day forecast for your area. Then keep a record of the actual weather that occurred. How close were the Weather Channel forecasters?

Teacher Plan

International Space Station

Before the Internet exercise

1. Discuss the history of the space program. Investigate your school media center, public library, or video store for a suitable videotape program.
2. Plan a trip to the media center to investigate the different phases of the United States space program. Have students prepare brief reports for the class.
3. Ask students to investigate the Skylab and Mir space stations. What do they have in common with the International Space Station? How are they different?

After the Internet exercise

1. Allow students to present their answers from the Kowabunga Dude! questions to the class. Post the results on a bulletin board.
2. Schedule a class debate on: "Is the International Space Station worth the cost?"
3. Ask students to design their own space stations. Students can make models or draw pictures. Display the designs in the classroom.

International Space Station

http://station.nasa.gov

1. Name the first element launched into space as part of the International Space Station.
2. What two countries have responsibility for providing launch vehicles for the International Space Station project?
3. When is the last mission currently scheduled for assembly of the International Space Station?
4. Name five areas of science that are planned for study at the International Space Station.
5. How many nations are members of the International Space Station project?
6. Several of the nations are members of the ESA. What do the letters ESA stand for?

From the "Frequently Asked Questions" section:

1. How many launches will be required to complete the International Space Station?
2. When will humans begin living on the International Space Station? How long will they live there?
3. What will be the altitude of the International Space Station?

Super Surfer

From the "Space Station History" section of this Web site (**http://station.nasa.gov/reference/history/**), research Noordung's Habitat Wheel. How realistic is this plan for the future? Write a brief report on the wheel and draw a picture of what you think the wheel would look like.

Kowabunga Dude!

1. Imagine that you have been selected to live on the International Space Station. You can take a small backpack filled with personal items. What would you take for the trip? Why?
2. Go to the section "Why a Space Station." Decide which reason is most valid and restate it in your own words.

Teacher Plan

NASA Astronaut Biographies

Before the Internet exercise

1. Conduct a class discussion in which students name famous astronauts. Ask the students to describe what they know and how they learned this information. Be prepared to provide prompts.
2. Ask the students to hypothesize about the requirements for becoming an astronaut. Have the students create a job description and/or a classified advertisement for an astronaut.

After the Internet exercise

1. Display the results of the Kowabunga Dude! activity on the bulletin board.
2. Discuss other types of exploring. What other adventures await people who are not astronauts (such as ocean exploring, mountain climbing, jungle safaris, etc.)? How are these adventures different and how are they similar to space exploration?
3. Divide the students into groups and have them create a five-day space shuttle mission. Ask the students to outline mission objectives and design activities that will fulfill those objectives.

NASA Astronaut Biographies

http://www.jsc.nasa.gov/Bios/astrobio.html

1. What is astronaut Terrence W. Wilcutt's current rank in the United States Marine Corps? Describe his duty in the service after he graduated from college.
2. On how many missions has astronaut Janice Voss flown?
3. How did astronaut Winston E. Scott serve his country before becoming a NASA astronaut?
4. Name astronaut Edward Lu's special fields of study.
5. When is astronaut Michael Lopez-Alegria's next space shuttle mission?
6. When was astronaut Tamara Jernigan's first space shuttle mission?
7. What was astronaut L. Blaine Hammond's job on STS-39? What is his current assignment?
8. Which two space shuttle flights did astronaut Michael Baker command?
9. Where did astronaut Kalpana Chawla earn her three college degrees?

From the "Additional Astronaut Information" page:

1. Using the "Wardrobe for Space" section, explain why humans must wear spacesuits while working in space. (There are two main reasons.)
2. What kinds of food are now available for astronauts to eat while on space shuttle missions?

Super Surfer

Follow the link to the question "How can I become an astronaut?" Make a list of the requirements for becoming a NASA astronaut.

Kowabunga Dude!

Imagine that you have been selected as a NASA astronaut. Using the biographies on this Web site, write your own biography as an astronaut. Consider attaching a school picture to your finished biography.

Teacher Plan

The Nine Planets

Before the Internet exercise

1. Facilitate a class discussion in which students list the nine planets of our solar system. Include descriptions of the planets. Ask the students to put the planets in order: size, distance from the sun, temperature, etc.
2. Ask the students to name planets that are visible: to the naked eye; using a simple telescope; using a professional telescope.
3. Access information about the Mars Pathfinder at **http://marsweb.jpl.nasa.gov/**. Ask students to describe our exploration of other planets.

After the Internet exercise

1. Create a model as described in the Kowabunga Dude! activity.
2. Use magazines, newspapers, and Web sites (try a Yahoo! search) to find more information about other planetary exploration missions.
3. Ask students to write a story about a trip to another planet. How long would it take to get there? What would they find? What obstacles would they encounter?
4. Ask students to imagine an alien that could live on a planet in our solar system. How would the alien survive under conditions that are extreme for humans?

The Nine Planets

http://seds.lpl.arizona.edu/nineplanets/nineplanets/nineplanets.html

1. What is the temperature on the surface of the sun?
2. The sun is composed mainly of two elements. Name them.
3. How old is the sun? How many more years will it continue in its present state?
4. Describe the surface of the planet Mercury.
5. What was the name of the first spacecraft to visit Venus? What year was that voyage?
6. What was the name of the most recent space vehicle to land on Mars?
7. What are the names of the two Martian moons?
8. Why is Jupiter called a "gas planet?"
9. How large is Jupiter's "Great Red Spot?"
10. What are Saturn's rings made of?
11. How many named satellites orbit Saturn? Which is the largest?
12. Who is given credit for discovering Uranus?
13. What is the composition of Uranus' atmosphere?
14. What is Neptune's most prominent feature? What happened to that feature?
15. Why do we know so little about Pluto? What is the name of Pluto's satellite?

Super Surfer

Go to "Appendix 7: Hypothetical Planets." Read one of the stories listed there. Rewrite the story in your own words and share your retelling with the class.

Kowabunga Dude!

Collect household objects that illustrate the relative sizes of the nine planets. Check out the "Overview of the Solar System" page for details. What is the biggest problem with the task of making a model of the solar system with real-world objects?

Teacher Plan

World Wildlife Fund

Before the Internet exercise

1 Lead a discussion about your students' favorite animals. Have the students seen the animals in person? How do they know about them? What do they like about them?

2. Lead a discussion about how environment effects animals. What would happen if an animal lost its habitat? How are animals different than people in this respect?

3. Lead a discussion of extinct animals. Students can use an encyclopedia to find animals that have become extinct in the 20th century.

After the Internet exercise

1. Identify local environmental groups and their efforts. Obtain literature from these groups.
2. Ask a member of a local environmental group to speak about local conservation activities.
3. Plan a school clean-up day. Inventory the litter collected, and hold a discussion about how to cut down on litter.
4. Identify several plant and animal species around your school. How do they depend on their environment to thrive?

World Wildlife Fund

http://www.wwf.org

1. According to the "Who We Are" section, how many countries are involved in the World Wildlife Fund's network?
2. Under "What We Do," find the five activities that the World Wildlife Fund undertakes.
3. According to the "Where Our Support Comes From" section, what is the largest source of operating revenue (money) for the World Wildlife Fund?
4. Using the bar graph provided, determine the amount of money that the WWF spent last year.
5. Find the "Top Ten Most Wanted List." Why are species on this list?
6. Select four of the species on the list. Tell why each species is in danger and what is being done to save it.
7. Select another area from the "Species at Risk" page. Describe the species, why it is at risk, and what is being done to save it.

Super Surfer

Select at least three of the countries in the "WWF Network" section. Visit these international Web sites. Try to determine what tasks these groups are undertaking (even though most of the sites are *not* in English!).

Kowabunga Dude!

Take at least one of the quizzes available on this Web site. Check your answers, and with the permission of your parent and/or teacher submit your answers to the WWF.

Teacher Plan

Caribbean Conservation Corporation/Sea Turtle Survival League

Before the Internet exercise

1. Ask students what they know about sea turtles. Make a list of the information on the board.
2. Visit the media center to conduct a research session about sea turtles. Assign each student a separate topic area (size, weight, habitat, diet, etc.). Encyclopedia, CD-ROM, print, and Internet sources can be used.
3. Divide the students into groups. Ask students to hypothesize how researchers track sea turtles. Each group should produce a drawing and make a class presentation.

After the Internet exercise

1. Florida has laws regulating human contact with sea turtles. Find the text of that law on the Internet. The Florida Statutes are on the World Wide Web at {**www.leg.state.fl.us**}. Print the law and discuss its impact on the sea turtles and the local communities.
2. Display the posters created in the Kowabunga Dude! activity.
3. Invite a member of a local environmental group to speak about local species and the steps that have been taken to protect them.

Caribbean Conservation Corporation/Sea Turtle Survival League

http://www.cccturtle.org

1. When was the Caribbean Conservation Corporation formed? Who founded it?
2. In what city is the CCC headquarters?
3. What kind of technology do researchers use to track the migration patterns of sea turtles?
4. What types of turtles were used in the migration/tracking study of 1997?
5. Why are only females used in the sea turtle migration/tracking study?
6. Where is the Archie Carr National Wildlife Refuge? How long is the beach there?
7. Name two characteristics of an area in which sea turtles will lay eggs.
8. What types of turtles use the Archie Carr National Wildlife Refuge?
9. When and where was Dr. Archie Carr born? At which university did he teach?
10. What five species of sea turtles are found in United States waters?
11. List the scientific classification for the loggerhead turtle. Include the kingdom, phylum, class, order, suborder, family, genus, and species.
12. How many eggs does the average sea turtle lay? How long do the eggs need to incubate before they hatch?
13. What are the chances of a baby sea turtle surviving into adulthood?

Super Surfer

Read the information on this Web site about watching nesting sea turtles. Make a list of rules that turtle watchers should follow.

Kowabunga Dude!

Make a poster using the information you discovered in the Super Surfer question. Take a photo of your poster and mail it to the Sea Turtle Survival League.

Teacher Plan

Sea World and Busch Gardens Animal Resources

Before the Internet exercise

1. Lead a class discussion on (and eventually provide the correct definitions of) the terms *order, family, genus,* and *species*.
2. Have students draw and/or collect pictures of animals, then sort the pictures by order, family, genus, and species.
3. Lead a discussion about your students' favorite animals. Why have they selected these animals?

After the Internet exercise

1. Invite a local animal care expert, veterinary worker, or zookeeper to speak about animals.
2. Visit the media center to collect information on animals. Each student can prepare a report following the format on this Web site. Prepare a template for students to follow.
3. Provide a forum for display and performance of the Kowabunga Dude! activity results.

Sea World and Busch Gardens Animal Resources Page

http://www.seaworld.org/infobook.html

1. What is the scientific classification of the beluga whale? (Include the order, the family, the genus, and the species.)
2. What do beluga whales eat? How much do they eat?
3. What is the bottlenose dolphin's habitat? In what oceans can it be found?
4. Which two of the bottlenose dolphin's senses are the best developed?
5. What is the average life span of a bottlenose dolphin?
6. What are the different colors of coral?
7. What are the two functions of tentacles in corals?
8. Name three reasons that corals and coral reefs are important to the environment.
9. What is the size (height and weight) of the typical male gorilla?
10. Why do gorillas have a pot-bellied appearance?
11. Name five ways that gorillas communicate their aggression.
12. How many different species of penguins are there? Name three of them.
13. In what parts of the world do penguins live?
14. Name three predators that prey on penguins.

Super Surfer

Investigate three of the careers listed in the "Zoological Park Careers" section. Write a brief summary of each career. Make sure to include the education and training needed.

Kowabunga Dude!

Select another species listed on this Web site and collect information on that species. Use the information to write a poem, compose a song, or draw a detailed picture of the animal that you select.

Teacher Plan

Worm World

Before the Internet exercise

1. Lead a discussion about the life of a worm. Ask the students to guess what a worm eats and how a worm moves. Write the answers on the board.
2. Bring some worms into the classroom. (You can probably buy worms at the local bait store.) Let the students "pet" the worms and hold them in the palms of their hands. Gently experiment with feeding a worm by hand. Ask the students to observe the different sizes of worms.
3. Let the students look at a live worm under a microscope. (You can also use a visual presenter or video camera with a macro lens.) Have students draw pictures of what they see.

After the Internet exercise

1. Following the directions on the "Worm World" Web site, create a classroom worm bin. A smaller bin can be made using a glass 10-gallon aquarium.
2. Look in the classified ad sections of gardening and natural living magazines. Several companies sell earthworms through the mail. Call one of these companies and ask for prices. Lead the class in a discussion: "Why would gardeners want to buy earthworms?"
3. Facilitate the student creations suggested in the Kowabunga Dude! section.

Worm World

http://www.nj.com/yucky/worm

1. Name the five worm "cousins" that are featured on the Web site.
2. Why are earthworms slimy?
3. How many years have worms been on Earth?
4. How many worms can live on one acre of land?
5. What are worm "castings" and what do they contain?
6. How big can South American earthworms grow?
7. What is another name for planaria?
8. Where do planaria live?

Worms as Recyclers

1. Name four living things that break down organic matter.
2. What do decomposers do?

Body Parts

1. How does a worm eat?
2. What does a worm use for teeth (since it doesn't have any)?

Super Surfer

Read "Amazing But True" facts in the "Fun Arcade" section. Write down the fact that you think is the most amazing. Compare your choice to your friends' choices.

Kowabunga Dude!

Draw a picture or write a poem about worms. With permission of your parent or teacher, submit your poem or artwork (either electronically or through the mail) to "Worm World." Instructions appear in the "Art Gallery" section of the Web site.

Teacher Plan

The Wolf Sanctuary

Before the Internet exercise

1. Ask the students what they know about wolves. List the characteristics they describe on the board.
2. Lead a discussion about different strategies used to save a species (protecting the environment versus protecting individual animals). Which strategies work best in different situations?

After the Internet exercise

1. Explore the wolf in legend and song. How is the wolf characterized in these stories and songs? (See, for example, Barbara Suwyn, *The Magic Egg and Other Tales from the Ukraine* (Libraries Unlimited, 1997) or Pelton and DiGennaro's *Images of a People* (Libraries Unlimited, 1997).)
2. Use a map to locate The Wolf Sanctuary. Is this area within the wolf's normal habitat? Use the information found during the Super Surfer activity to find the locations of other wolf sanctuaries.
3. Write letters to one or more of the wolf organizations found on this and other Web sites. Ask for a brochure or pamphlet that describes the group's activities.

The Wolf Sanctuary

http://www.wolfsanctuary.org

1. What is the name of the research center that serves as the location of The Wolf Sanctuary?
2. When was The Wolf Sanctuary founded? Who was the main founder?
3. What are the main goals of The Wolf Sanctuary?
4. Which wolf species are bred at The Wolf Sanctuary?
5. How many acres of land does The Wolf Sanctuary include?
6. What do the wolves at The Wolf Sanctuary eat?
7. If you visit The Wolf Sanctuary, can you pet the wolves? Why or why not?
8. What is the main reason that wolves are on the brink of extinction?

From the "Wolf Factoids" section (under "Facts and Information"):

1. How many teeth does a wolf have?
2. Why do wolves howl?
3. What are the two species of wolves?

Super Surfer

Visit one of the sites listed in the "Wolf Sanctuary's Links to the World" section. Describe the efforts of that organization. Prepare a brief report and present it to the class.

Kowabunga Dude!

Find out if wolves populate your area, or if they ever populated the area in which you now live. Use reference books, Internet resources, and personal interviews to find your results.

Teacher Plan

The Tiger Information Center

Before the Internet exercise

1. Ask students if they have ever seen a tiger (in person). Where did they see the tiger?
2. Visit your school media center, community library, or local video rental store and obtain an age-appropriate video on tigers. Show the video to the class.
3. Many people are intrigued by tigers. Lead a class discussion about this attraction.
4. Identify the tiger as an element in legends and folklore. In which countries are tigers part of the heritage? (Two useful resources are Norma Livo and Dia Cha, *Folk Stories of the Hmong* (Libraries Unlimited, 1997) and Supaporn Vathanaprida, *Thai Tales* (Libraries Unlimited, 1997).)

After the Internet exercise

1. Use a map to locate the tiger habitats described on this Web site.
2. Ask a zookeeper or local animal expert to speak about tigers.
3. Conduct a discussion about extinction. Why did many tigers become extinct? Why is the tiger population threatened today?

The Tiger Information Center

http://www.5tigers.org

1. What are the five tiger subspecies that are alive today?
2. On what continent do tigers live in the wild today?
3. How many tigers remain in the wild?
4. Name three tiger subspecies that have become extinct in the past 70 years.
5. How many Siberian tigers exist in the wild? How many Siberian tigers are in zoos?
6. According to the "Size Variation in Tiger Subspecies" chart, which tiger weighs the most? Which tiger is the smallest?
7. Describe a tiger's night vision.
8. Why do tigers scratch on trees?
9. How long can a tiger in the wild expect to live?
10. How much meat can a wild tiger eat at one time?
11. What are the three main threats to tigers in the wild?

From the "Common Misconceptions about Tigers" section:

1. Most cats do not like water. Do tigers?

Super Surfer

Using the resources of this Web site, locate the three zoos closest to you that have tigers on display. What types of tigers do they have?

Kowabunga Dude!

Read the "How You Can Help Tigers" section. Make a list of things you can do to protect tigers.

Teacher Plan

The Cat Fanciers' Association

Before the Internet exercise

1. Lead a class discussion about cats. What do the students know about cats? Which students have pet cats? Ask students to bring photos of their pet cats.
2. Lead a discussion: "Why do people like cats? Why do cats make good pets for some people?"
3. Plan a media center visit to research cats. What roles have cats played in the history of some cultures and societies?

After the Internet exercise

1. Ask a local veterinarian or other animal care expert to speak about the proper care of cats.
2. Ask an animal shelter or Humane Society worker to speak about the cat population.
3. Students can draw pictures of their favorite cats found on this Web site. Display the pictures on the bulletin board.

The Cat Fanciers' Association

http://www.cfainc.org

1. According to this Web site, what is the Cat Fanciers' Association?
2. For the most recent show season, which breed of cat was named

   The "Best Cat?"

   The "Best Kitten?"

   The "Best Cat in Premiership?"
3. From the "Caring for Cats" section, correct the following cat myths in your own words.

   "Cats always land on their feet."

   "Cats should drink milk everyday."

   "Cats cannot get rabies."

   "A cat's sense of balance is in its whiskers."

   "Animals heal themselves by licking their wounds."
4. You may want to enter your household pet in a CFA cat show. What are the four standards for judging a household pet cat?
5. How many breeds are listed and described on this Web site?

Super Surfer

Visit the Web site of the American Kennel Club (**http://www.akc.org**). Compare the two sites. Which topics addressed by the AKC Web site do not appear on the CFA Web site?

Kowabunga Dude!

Read the description of the Selkirk Rex cat that appears on this Web site. Then read an encyclopedia entry about genetics. Make a chart that illustrates the development of this breed.

Teacher Plan

FitLife

Before the Internet exercise

1. Lead a class discussion about healthy lifestyles. Determine what students do in their spare time. List the most common activities on the board.
2. Assign a time-activity log as a student activity. Have students keep track of all of their time for two or three days. Then have students examine their completed logs, searching for physical fitness activities.
3. Discuss physical fitness. How can a person become more physically fit? What choices must be made?

After the Internet exercise

1. Invite a doctor or other medical professional to speak about the importance of living a healthy life.
2. Discuss the concept of wellness as described on this Web site. List several activities that would be considered wellness activities.
3. Have students draw a picture or write a poem about a fitness activity or lifestyle.

FitLife

http://fitlife.com

1. "Wellness" is the opposite of _____________.
2. The terms "health promotion" and "wellness" include a variety of general behaviors and lifestyle activities that help _________ _________ __________ and _________.
3. In the section "Effective Eating for Those Who Exercise" you will find the food pyramid. Restate the food pyramid in your own words.
4. What food groups contain complex carbohydrates?
5. Are foods that are low in fat necessarily low in calories? Give an example to support your answer.
6. According to this Web site, how many glasses of water should a person drink each day?
7. Why is drinking water important for people who want to lose weight?
8. Is skipping meals a good idea if you want to lose weight? Why or why not?
9. Is stress always bad? Why or why not?
10. What should a person do before beginning a physical fitness program?
11. Effective training can be described with the letters FIT. What do these three letters stand for? What are the three phases of training?

Super Surfer

1. The Federal Government Catalog, which lists several nutritional pamphlets, is available on request. Write, call, or e-mail your request. (Check the "Consumer Information Online" section on the Web site.)
2. Contribute a recipe to the "FitLife" recipe section.

Kowabunga Dude!

The American Council on Science and Health recently rated several nutrition magazines. Their findings are listed on this Web site. Find an issue of one of those magazines and evaluate it yourself.

Teacher Plan

The American Lung Association: "Learn About Lung Health"

Before the Internet exercise

1. Lead a class discussion about air quality. Why is air quality difficult to define?
2. Make a list of activities that harm the quality of the air. Students may enjoy working in groups for this activity.
3. Investigate air quality issues, laws, and standards in your area.

After the Internet exercise

1. Contact the local office of the American Lung Association, or any other agency interested in air quality. Ask for a guest speaker to visit your classroom.
2. Have students survey family members about their smoking habits. When did they begin? When/how did they stop? What first attracted them to cigarettes?
3. Investigate other American Lung Association activities as described on this Web site. Make a list of their efforts.

The American Lung Association: "Learn About Lung Health"

http://www.lungusa.org/index2.html

1. How many Americans suffer from asthma?
2. Name four common asthma and allergy "triggers."
3. Asthma is considered a chronic disease. What does this mean?
4. List four common symptoms of asthma.
5. How many children in the United States suffer from asthma?
6. According to the Web site, how many Americans die each year from smoking-related diseases?
7. What is the value (in dollars) of the health care cost and lost productivity due to smoking?
8. In your own words, define *second-hand smoke*.
9. List three ways that you can protect yourself and your family from second-hand smoke.
10. What is the addictive drug found in tobacco?
11. Besides addiction, name four reasons why people become hooked on smoking.
12. Name three diseases associated with cigarette smoking.

Super Surfer

List six major air pollutants as described by the United States Environmental Protection Agency. (Note: this answer can be found without leaving the American Lung Association Web site.)

Kowabunga Dude!

With permission of your parent or teacher, call the American Lung Association toll-free phone number listed on this Web site. Ask for information on the "Freedom from Smoking" project.

Teacher Plan

Fruit and Vegetable Nutrition Center

Before the Internet exercise

1. Ask students to name fruits and vegetables. Write their answers on the board. Have them name as many fruits and vegetables as they can!
2. Visit the local supermarket and purchase several uncommon fruits and vegetables. Share these with your students. Ask how they would prepare them.
3. Ask students to hypothesize which countries grow the most fruit. Check the answers later when visiting this Web site.
4. Assign a fruit/vegetable diary. Students should write each serving of fruits and vegetables that they eat each day.

After the Internet exercise

1. Assign a country to each student. Ask the student to write a paragraph describing the fruits and vegetables produced by that country.
2. Determine what fruits and vegetables are grown in your area. Why are these crops grown there?
3. Have students bring seeds from fresh fruits and vegetables. Start a small garden at school.
4. Ask the produce manager of a local supermarket or fruit-and-vegetable market to speak about fruits and vegetables. Make sure he or she describes how the crops get from the fields to the market shelves.

Fruit and Vegetable Nutrition Center

http://www.dole5aday.com/nut_center/NUTINFO.html

1. Apples are a good source of ____________________.
2. How many calories are in a medium-sized banana?
3. How many grams of fat are in a serving of cantaloupe?
4. How many grams of protein can be found in a serving of broccoli?
5. How many calories are found in a serving of eggplant?
6. What percentage of the daily requirement of iron can be found in a serving of spinach?
7. Name one fruit and two vegetables that have at least 100% of the daily requirement of Vitamin A in each serving.
8. Name one fruit and one vegetable that have more than 100% of the daily requirement of Vitamin C in each serving.
9. In your words, what does "Eat Five a Day Everyday" mean?

Super Surfer

From the Nutrition Facts page about grapes, go to the "Cool Stuff about Chilean Fruit" page.

1. Write the Spanish word for each of the following fruits:

   Grapes Nectarines Raspberries
   Pears Plums

2. What is the main form of transportation used to get fruit from Chile to the United States? How long does this trip take?

Kowabunga Dude!

Make a fruit or vegetable salad. Team up with two or three class members. Each member should bring a serving of a vegetable or fruit (serving size can be found on the Web site). Combine your fruits or vegetables in a bowl to make a fruit or vegetable salad. Use the information on this Web site to determine the nutritional value of your salad. Make sure to include all of the important information. Then eat your salad!

Teacher Plan

Fast Food Facts—Interactive Food Finder

Before the Internet exercise

1. Lead a class discussion about the fast food restaurants in your area. Make a list on the board. Ask students which fast food restaurants are their favorites and what they like about them.
2. Have the students describe their favorite fast food meals and their favorite home-cooked meals. (This can be done in paragraph form.) Then have the students compare and contrast these two meals. How are they prepared? What are the main ingredients? How are they served? How do you feel after you've eaten?

After the Internet exercise

1. Ask a nutritionist or other nutrition expert to speak to the class about proper eating habits.
2. Invite the physical education teacher to speak to the class about exercise. He or she can lead the class in exercises that will help burn those fast food calories!

Fast Food Facts—Interactive Food Finder

http://www.olen.com/food/

1. This Web site is based on a book called *Fast Food Facts*. Who produced this book?
2. Imagine that you're in Burger King and you want a sandwich that has 400 calories or less. Name two choices that you have.
3. What sandwiches can you eat at Burger King if you want to limit your fat intake to fewer than 12 grams?
4. At Hardees, you decide to order a Big Deluxe hamburger, a medium order of french fries, and a vanilla shake. How many calories will you be eating? How many grams of fat will you be eating?
5. Compare the meal in question #4 with the calories and grams of fat from a Hardees chef salad with a glass of water. Which has more, and by how much?
6. You're at Taco Bell and you want to limit your calorie intake. List a few wise menu choices for your meal.
7. At Subway, list three 6-inch subs that have 400 or fewer calories and less than 20 grams of fat.
8. At McDonald's, how can a person unintentionally add sodium to an order of Chicken McNuggets?
9. Which McDonald's sandwich is highest in calories and sodium?

Super  Surfer

Compare Burger King's Whopper to McDonald's Quarter-Pounder with Cheese. (Compare calories, grams of fat, sodium, and cholesterol.)

Kowabunga Dude!

Call or visit your favorite fast food restaurant. Ask them to name the items included in their best-selling meal. Use this Web site to determine the calories, fat grams, cholesterol, and sodium content of the meal. Then design a healthier meal based on the restaurant's menu.

Teacher Plan

On Broadway—WWW Information Page

Before the Internet exercise

1. Ask students about plays they have seen and plays in which they have performed. Make a list on the board.
2. Obtain a map of New York City. Find Broadway on that map.
3. Lead a discussion: Why is it important for an actor to make it to Broadway?

After the Internet exercise

1. What does "making it to Broadway" say about an actor's career? List the equivalents to Broadway in other fields (performing arts, sports, medicine, etc.).
2. Have each student create a poster for a Broadway play described on this site. Display the posters around the room.
3. Invite a local actor, director, or drama instructor to speak about Broadway and the professional theater.

On Broadway—WWW Information Page

http://artsnet.heinz.cmu.edu/OnBroadway/pages/Main.html

1. From the "Current Listings" section, name three plays that are currently on Broadway. For each play, list the play's name, the director, the name of the theater, and the price for a ticket to the play.
2. From the "Current Listings Off Broadway" section, name three plays that are currently running off-Broadway. For each play, list the play's name, the play's director, the name of the theater, and the price for a ticket to the play.
3. In "Broadway History" select "The Tony Awards." For whom is the Tony Award named?
4. What year were the first Tony Awards given? Who won the award for Outstanding Playwright that year?
5. For the most recent year:

   Which play won Best Play?

   Which play won Best Musical?

   Who won Best Actor in a Play and Best Actress in a Play?

   Who won Best Actor in a Musical and Best Actress in a Musical?

Super  Surfer

1. Follow the "Theatre Links" hyperlink. You will find links to Web sites of individual plays. Select a Web site and write a brief summary of what you find.
2. Several play reviews can be found on this Web site. Read a review and summarize it in your own words. What did the critic like? What did the critic dislike? If you were an actor in this play, would you consider it a good review or a bad review?

Kowabunga Dude!

Imagine that a school play produced recently at your school has made it to Broadway. Create a listing for your school's play following the format for listings on this Web site. Make sure to include who wrote the play, a brief summary of the play, the performance schedule, and the price of tickets.

Teacher Plan

The History of Superhero Comic Books

Before the Internet exercise

1. Lead a discussion about comic books. Make a list of the students' favorite comics and what they like about them (make sure to distinguish between comics that students actually read and those that they have heard other students talk about).
2. Ask a comic book shop owner to speak to the class about his or her experiences in the comic book industry.
3. Lead a class discussion about comic book infiltration in other media. What comic characters have appeared in movies and television shows?
4. Lead a class discussion: Why are comic books popular? Write the answers on the board.

After the Internet exercise

1. Ask students to share the superheroes that they have created in the Kowabunga Dude! activity. Display the artwork.
2. Extend the Kowabunga Dude! activity by putting students in groups and assigning the task of creating a comic book based on all of their superhero creations.
3. Ask a local comic book artist, cartoonist, or art teacher to speak to the class about comic strips and comic books. (Note: many local newspapers have their own cartoonists or artist who may be able to help you in this activity.)

The History of Superhero Comic Books

http://www.geocities.com/Athens/8580/Hist1.html

1. What was the name of the "funny book" that was published in 1896?
2. According to the author, what was the name of the first "true comic book" and how much did it cost?
3. What was different about *New Fun Comics* published in 1935?
4. What was the name of the comic book in which Superman first appeared?
5. What crime-fighting hero first appeared in *Detective Comics* #27?
6. Which character was featured in the first Marvel comic?
7. The very first sidekick appeared in *Detective Comics* #38. What was his name, and whom did he assist?
8. What was the name of the first comic book superhero team, and in which comic book did they appear?
9. Who was Captain America's enemy in the early 1940s?
10. Which popular character was featured in *Pep Comics* #22?

Super Surfer

Why was Wonder Woman an important character in 1940s comic books? How did she compare with established female role models of the time?

Kowabunga Dude!

Design your own superhero. What is his or her name? What special powers does he or she have? Sketch your creation!

Teacher Plan

Carnegie Hall

Before the Internet exercise

1. Ask students to name concerts that they have attended and in which they have performed. How did they feel about performing music in front of an audience?
2. On a map of New York City, find Carnegie Hall. What other landmarks are in the vicinity?
3. Lead a discussion (or assign a report) on acoustics. Which surfaces absorb sound? Which reflect it? List real-life situations (such as "singing in the shower") and ask students to describe the acoustics.

After the Internet exercise

1. Contact a local community college, college, or university with a theater department. Ask the theater manager to speak about his or her job. (Perhaps this activity could be part of a field trip to the theater.)
2. Display the posters created in the Kowabunga Dude! activity.
3. Have students design a concert hall. They should include all of the important elements, such as seating, stage, box office, backstage area, dressing rooms, exits, etc.

Carnegie Hall

http://www.carnegiehall.org/main.html

1. From the "Carnegie Hall—Then and Now" section: What year was Carnegie Hall opened?
2. Who first had the idea to build Carnegie Hall? Who was his son, who continued his work?
3. A wealthy businessman provided financial support to build Carnegie Hall. Who was this businessman and what business was he in?
4. Who was the architect for Carnegie Hall? What corner property was obtained to build Carnegie Hall?
5. Which famous composer conducted the orchestra on the first opening night at Carnegie Hall?
6. Which tradition did Walter Damrosch begin at Carnegie Hall?
7. In 1995, rock performer Sting hosted a benefit concert at Carnegie Hall. Which charity benefited from the concert? Name three other musicians who performed that night.
8. From the "New and Notable" section: What season "number" is Carnegie Hall currently in?
9. Name at least three musicians who will be playing at upcoming Carnegie Hall concerts. List the instruments they play.

Super Surfer

1. Under the "Services Guide," visit the page for the Rose Museum. Write a brief history of the Rose Museum.
2. How many people can be seated in the different sections of Carnegie Hall? (Hint: the answer can be found as part of the "Services Guide.")

Kowabunga Dude!

Imagine that your school musical group has been invited to perform at Carnegie Hall. Make a poster advertising the concert. Make sure to list the location of Carnegie Hall and how much you will charge for tickets.

Teacher Plan

Medieval and Renaissance Instruments

Before the Internet exercise

1. Ask students to name musical instruments. Which instruments can they play? How did they learn?
2. Lead a class discussion: Why do people invent musical instruments?
3. Assign as a paragraph or a group discussion topic: Imagine that you want to invent a new musical instrument. What raw materials that are found in your area could you use? What type of instrument would you make?

After the Internet exercise

1. Ask a local school band director to speak to the class about musical instruments. Ask him or her to bring several music students to demonstrate their musical instruments.
2. Obtain a varicty of musical recordings from your local public library. Play selections for the class and ask students to identify the instruments used.
3. Assign an oral or written report on some aspect of medieval/renaissance life. Have students share their reports with the class.

Medieval and Renaissance Instruments

http://www.s-hamilton.k12.ia.us/antiqua/instrumt.html

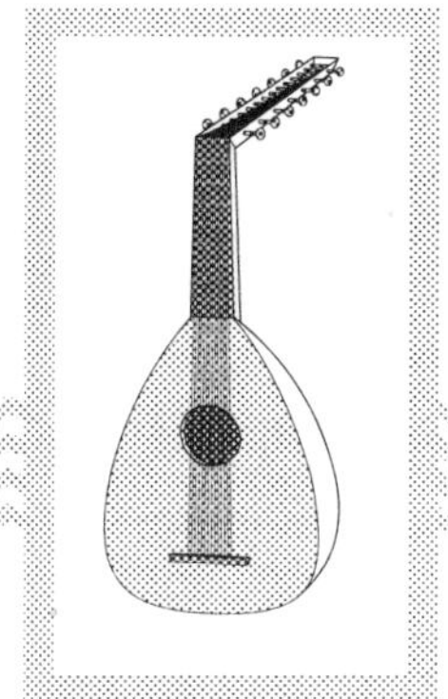

1. What group of workers probably invented the bagpipe?
2. How did the crumhorn get its name?
3. How is a dulcimer played?
4. From what material is a gemshorn made?
5. What were three materials used to make strings for the harp in the Middle Ages?
6. Why did a large hurdy-gurdy made before 1300 require two musicians?
7. Describe the shape of the lizard.
8. Name at least three types of wood used to make a lute.
9. How is the wind supplied to make the music of the organetto?
10. Which modern instrument does a sacbut resemble? What is the literal translation of "sacbut"?
11. What common band instrument evolved from the serpent?
12. From which ancient culture did the shofar descend? What two animal horns were used to make shofars?

Super Surfer

Follow the link at the bottom of the page to the group "Musica Antiqua." Write a brief report about this group.

Kowabunga Dude!

Invent your own musical instrument. Draw a picture and write a brief description of it. Make sure to tell how it is held, what it sounds like, and from what materials it could be made.

Teacher Plan

The National Park Service ParkNet

Before the Internet exercise

1. Lead a discussion: Why do we have parks? Why are they important? What would be lost if we did not have parks?
2. Make a list of the parks in your area. Determine if they are city parks, county parks, state parks, or national parks.
3. Assign a brief report on the history and development of national parks. Plan a media center visit to facilitate the research.

After the Internet exercise

1. Invite the ranger or supervisor of a local park to speak to the class about his or her job.
2. Assign an investigation of the history of local parks. When did they begin? Who founded them?
3. Have students design a poster for a local or national park. They should include important information such as the location, activities, hours of operation, and fees. (Information can be obtained from this Web site, or from local sources.) Display the posters in the classroom or in the media center.
4. Assign students to write letters to the editor of the local newspaper on the importance of parks.

The National Park Service ParkNet

http://www.nps.gov

In the "Visit Your Parks" section, use the "Find a Park" function to answer the following questions:

1. Near what city would you find the Abraham Lincoln Birthplace National Historic Site?
2. How many people visit Badlands National Park each year? At what time of year is the park least crowded?
3. Name three other attractions in the area of the Washington Monument.
4. What are three exhibits that can be seen at the Tuskegee Institute National Historic Site?
5. What world record distinction is held by Rainbow Bridge?
6. How many petroglyphs can be found at Petroglyph National Monument? What is a petroglyph?
7. Which four presidents are carved into Mount Rushmore?
8. What famous events in the creation of the United States of America took place at what is now Independence National Historic Park?
9. At Hawaii Volcanoes National Park a visitor can see the earth's most massive volcano and the world's most active volcano. What are the names of these two volcanoes?
10. Use the state map to find the names of the three national parks closest to your home.

Super Surfer

Visit the Web site of the Park of the Month. Write a brief report on the site. Include the location of the park, the climate, and some of the activities of the park.

Kowabunga Dude!

Select one of the parks and plan a three-day trip there. Plan your transportation, what clothes to pack, and where you would sleep. Make a list of the items you would take with you.

Teacher Plan

The United States Show Caves Directory

Before the Internet exercise

1. From your school media center, public library, or video rental store, obtain an age-appropriate film or video about caves. Show the video to the class.
2. Invite a local geologist or science teacher/professor to speak on how caves are formed.
3. Lead a class discussion: What is a show cave? How do they differ from other caves and caverns?
4. Lead a class discussion: Why are people interested in cave exploration?

After the Internet exercise

1. Locate several of the caves mentioned on this Web site on a United States map.
2. Display and share the products of the Kowabunga Dude! activity.
3. Does your community have a local cave-exploration or spelunking club? If so, ask a member to speak with the class. Make sure he or she brings some caving equipment.

The United States Show Caves Directory

http://www.goodearth.com/showcave.html

1. According to the "Why Visit Show Caves" section, what is the longest cave in the world?
2. Near what city can you find Florida Caverns State Park?
3. Why is Florida Caverns not a typical Florida cave?
4. Lehman Cave in Nevada features several cave shields. What is a cave shield? How are they formed?
5. How large is the Big Room at New Mexico's Carlsbad Caverns National Park?
6. California's Boyden Cavern is located in the deepest canyon in the United States. What is the name of the canyon? How deep is it? How long did it take for nature to create Boyden Cavern?
7. At Blanchard Springs Cavern in Arkansas, which tour is accessible to visitors in wheelchairs?
8. How did South Dakota's Jewel Cave National Monument get its name?
9. Why is the cave at Wind Cave National Park described as a "natural barometer"?

Super Surfer

Take this Web site's Virtual Cave Tour. Observe at least five cave features on this tour. Write a brief report on these features.

Kowabunga Dude!

Make a list of safety tips that you would follow in a cave. Make a drawing or compose a poem featuring these safety tips.

Teacher Plan

The Official Site of the Negro Baseball Leagues

Before the Internet exercise

1. Lead a discussion about the existence of the Negro Baseball Leagues.
2. Lead a discussion: Why was there a separate baseball league for African Americans? Make sure to include information about civil rights for minorities in the 1930s, 1940s, and 1950s.

After the Internet exercise

1. Contact a local African American organization. Invite a guest speaker who recalls the Negro Baseball Leagues to share his or her memories.
2. Lead an investigation of barriers to minority participation in other professional sports.

The Official Site of the Negro Baseball Leagues

http://www.majorleaguebaseball.com/nbl/index.sml

1. When were the Negro Baseball Leagues founded? Why were they founded?

From the "History" section:

1. Name three players in the National Baseball Hall of Fame (Cooperstown) who played in the Negro Baseball Leagues.
2. Where is the Negro Baseball Leagues Museum? When did the museum open? What Negro Baseball Leagues team played in this city?

From the "Teams" section:

1. What fantastic record did The Grays establish from 1937–1945?
2. Which major league baseball home run king played for the Birmingham Black Barons during their last championship season?

From the "Players" section:

1. How much money did Walter "Buck" Leonard make as a professional baseball player in 1934?
2. With which major league baseball team did Jackie Robinson sign? Why was this an important event?

Super Surfer

Visit the Negro Baseball Leagues Shop page. What happens to the proceeds from the sale of this merchandise?

Kowabunga Dude!

Plan a visit to the Negro Baseball Leagues Museum. How would you get there? What could you expect to see in the museum? What other attractions are in the area?

Teacher Plan

The All-American Girls Professional Baseball League

Before the Internet exercise

1. Lead a class discussion on the current state of women's professional sports. Which sports feature professional women athletes? Which sports are still male-dominated? Are any sports female-dominated?
2. Lead a discussion: Why are women's sports emerging in the 1990s?

After the Internet exercise

1. Invite a local college or professional female athlete to speak to the class.
2. Lead a class exploration on laws and regulations requiring equal access to sports for women. How has this affected school sports?
3. Assign brief reports on women athletes. Have students share the information with the class.

The All-American Girls Professional Baseball League

http://www.dlcwest.com/~smudge/contents.html

1. What years was the All-American Girls Professional Baseball League in existence?
2. Who invented the All-American Girls Professional Baseball League? What major league baseball team did he own?
3. What was the key factor in the league's disbanding?
4. According to the "Player Roster" section, how many players played in the All-American Girls Professional Baseball League?
5. Name the four teams that participated in the All-American Girls Professional Baseball League's first season.
6. Which season had the most teams participating?
7. What was the highest batting average recorded in the All-American Girls Professional Baseball League? Who was the player, and what year did she record that average?
8. Which team won the first All-American Girls Professional Baseball League championship? Which team won the last championship?
9. Who wrote the "Victory Song" of the All-American Girls Professional Baseball League?
10. How many bases did Sophie Kurys steal in her career?

Super Surfer

Read the "Rules of Conduct for Players" on the Baseball Trivia Page. Write a one-paragraph reaction.

Kowabunga Dude!

Make a list of professional sports that were formerly played only by men. What opportunities exist today for women in these sports?

Teacher Plan

A Guide to the Great Sioux Nation

Before the Internet exercise

1. Lead a discussion about Native Americans. What do we know? How do we know it?
2. Locate the area known as the Northern Plains on a United States map.
3. What Native American tribes once lived in your area? Which tribes still make an impact?

After the Internet exercise

1. Assign a Native American word to each student. Have the student draw a picture depicting this word. Use *Indian Terms of the Americas* by Patterson and Snodgrass (Libraries Unlimited, 1994) as a resource.
2. Invite a local Native American or local historian to talk about Native American life.

A Guide to the Great Sioux Nation

http://www.state.sd.us/state/executive/tourism/sioux/sioux.htm

1. What modern-day American state is featured in this description of the Sioux Nation?
2. What were the three dialects spoken in the Great Sioux Nation?
3. In 1800 the Great Sioux Nation dominated the North Plains. Name the five present-day states that make up the land formerly inhabited by the Sioux.
4. In the 1860s, why did Red Cloud fight to close the Bozeman Trail?
5. What was discovered in 1874 that encouraged non-natives to move into the Black Hills?
6. What famous American general was defeated on June 25, 1876, by the Sioux and the Cheyenne?
7. What was the Lakota Sioux name for the Black Hills?
8. Describe the geography of the Badlands.
9. Which member of the Sioux Nation is featured in a mountain carving in the Black Hills? How big will the carving be when it is completed?
10. What animal did the Sioux women use to create unique clothing and accessories?
11. What is the Sioux word for "powwow"?
12. Name three foods that can be found at a Sioux powwow.
13. Name two times that everyone should stand when visiting a Sioux powwow.

Super Surfer

List the nine tribes of the Great Sioux Nation. Name a leader of each tribe and the major accomplishment for which the leader is known.

Kowabunga Dude!

Call one of the Sioux museums and ask them to send you a brochure. (These are all long-distance telephone calls. Make sure to ask a parent or teacher before calling.)

Teacher Plan

J. P. Morgan & Co. Holiday Calendar

Before the Internet exercise

1. Lead a discussion: Why are holidays important? Make a list of reasons on the board.
2. Select a few of the holidays from question #1. What are the origins of these holidays? Are they religious, cultural, or government holidays?
3. Lead a discussion: Which holidays would you expect to be the same in all countries? Which holidays would be different?

After the Internet exercise

1. Discuss the various holidays that students have found in this exercise.
2. Combine all of the students' findings and create an international calendar of holidays. You may want to use a desktop publishing computer program to help make the calendar.
3. Have students perform an Alta Vista search on the holiday of their choice. How many Web sites are there about their holiday?

J. P. Morgan & Co. Holiday Calendar

http://www.jpmorgan.com/cgi-bin/HolidayCalendar

1. Write today's date. Is there a holiday in the world today? If so, list it.
2. Write the names of five countries of the world. For each country that you have selected, use the "Holidays by Country" function to find and list at least three holidays celebrated by that country.
3. List holidays similar to the holidays celebrated in the United States. (For example, many nations celebrate New Year's Day, although they may not agree on the date!)
4. Write five dates (example: May 12th). You can use your birthday and/or any other dates that mean something to you, or you can just select dates at random. Use the "Holidays on a Particular Day" section to find holidays around the world on your five dates. (You may have to pick new dates if no holidays are on your selections.) Try to list at least three countries and their holidays for each date that you chose.

Super Surfer

The J. P. Morgan Company sponsors this page. Follow the site's hyperlink to the company home page.

1. What type of business is the J. P. Morgan Company involved in?
2. Why do you think it would be important for their employees to have access to information about world holidays?

Kowabunga Dude!

Use an encyclopedia, reference book, CD-ROM, or Web site to research a holiday that you didn't know about before today. Try to find out how and why that holiday is celebrated. Present your findings to the class.

Teacher Plan

Kanazawa City

Before the Internet exercise

1. Locate Japan on a map or globe. Locate Kanazawa and other major cities.
2. Lead a discussion: Why would a city have a Web page?
3. List Japanese contributions to American life (include food, business, arts, etc.).
4. Lead a discussion: How does a city's geography affect its citizens' lifestyles?

After the Internet exercise

1. Find newspaper and magazine articles about Japan. Create a bulletin board using these articles.
2. Find other Japanese cities on the World Wide Web. Perform a Yahoo! or Alta Vista search. How do the Web sites compare?
3. Have students research Japanese food. How does it differ from other oriental cuisine (Chinese, Korean, Vietnamese, etc.)?
4. Does your city have a Web site? If so, invite the Web site developer to speak about the Web site. Why did the city place the site on the Web? What has it gained from the Internet presence?

Kanazawa City

http://www.city.kanazawa.ishikawa.jp/kanazawaE.html

1. In what Japanese district would you find Kanazawa City?
2. What year was Kanazawa City founded?
3. Kanazawa City was formerly a "castle town." What was the name of the feudal Japanese clan that built a castle there?
4. How many people live in Kanazawa City?
5. What is the name of the mountain range that surrounds Kanazawa City?
6. What two national parks are in the area?
7. What two rivers run through Kanazawa City?
8. What is the hottest month of the year in Kanazawa City? What is the average temperature then?
9. Name the six skills associated with "the Way" in Japan.
10. What kind of craftwork is associated with the following terms?

    Kaga Yuzen   Noh   Kanazawa Shikki   Kanazawa Haku   Ohiyaki
11. Name Kanazawa City's six "sister cities."
12. Who is the mayor of Kanazawa City?

Super Surfer

Go to the "Old Customs" section of this page. Select one of the festivals listed and write a paragraph about that festival.

Kowabunga Dude!

Visit the "Communications Spot" featured on this Web site. With your teacher's or parent's permission, compose a note about your class study of this Web site and submit it on-line!

Teacher Plan

United Nations Home Page

Before the Internet exercise

1. Lead a class discussion about the time frame of the founding of the United Nations. What else was happening in the world at that time?
2. Talk to the students about the League of Nations and its place in United Nations history.
3. Lead a class discussion: Why is it important to have a forum in which the world can discuss conflicts and ideas?
4. Ask students to bring in current newspaper and magazine articles about the United Nations. Make a bulletin board featuring the articles.

After the Internet exercise

1. Discuss the Kowabunga Dude! activity. Make an agenda for a United Nations meeting. You may wish to role-play an actual UN session.
2. Hold a class debate: Is the United Nations worth the cost?

United Nations Home Page

http://www.un.org

1. When did the United Nations officially come into existence?
2. Who is the current United Nations secretary-general? What country is he or she from?
3. Who was the first United Nations secretary-general?
4. How many member states are in the United Nations?
5. Who are the five permanent member countries of the United Nations Security Council?
6. Where does the International Court of Justice hold court?
7. In what city is the United Nations headquarters located?
8. What is a United Nations peacekeeping operation?
9. How many United Nations peacekeeping operations have there been since 1945?
10. Who is in charge of the United Nations peacekeeping operations?
11. What United Nations division creates laws of the oceans?
12. Write the full names of the following United Nations divisions. Briefly summarize their missions.

    UNEP UNDRO UNICEF WFP WHO

Super Surfer

From the "Economic and Social Development" page, select one topic area that interests you. Follow the link to the appropriate United Nations page and then write a paragraph about United Nations efforts on that topic.

Kowabunga Dude!

Imagine that you are a delegate to the United Nations. Make a list of topics that you think the nations of the world should discuss.

Teacher Plan

THOMAS—U.S. Congress on the Internet

Before the Internet exercise

1. Obtain a copy of the videotape "I'm Just a Bill," an installment of ABC's Schoolhouse Rock series. Share the segment with your class. (Even the older students will find it entertaining.)
2. Ask students to bring in newspaper clippings of bills under consideration by the U.S. Congress. Make a bulletin board using the clippings.
3. Lead a class discussion: Why are laws important?
4. Lead a class discussion: Why do we have a representative government? How can we contact our representatives? (This is an excellent time for students to discover which congressional district they live in.)

After the Internet exercise

1. Ask students about their ideas for new national laws. Encourage students to write their representatives about these issues.
2. Ask a local lawmaker (or one of their office staff members) to speak to the class.
3. Lead a class discussion: In addition to this Web site, what are other ways that citizens can stay informed about bills and laws?

THOMAS—U.S. Congress on the Internet

http://thomas.loc.gov

1. For which American patriot is this Web site named?
2. What "number" Congress is currently in session? (Example: 104th Congress)
3. List the titles of three bills that were discussed or voted on in the Senate or the House of Representatives this week.
4. Name three documents currently in the Historical Documents Collection.
5. Use the "Bills by Topic" section to find current or recent bills about the following subjects. Write the name and number for each bill.

    Criminal Justice

    Job Training

    Transportation

Super Surfer

List the chairperson of each of the following congressional committees:

The Senate Committee on Agriculture, Nutrition, and Forestry

The Senate Committee on Environment and Public Works

The Senate Committee on Labor and Human Resources

The House Committee on Education and the Workforce

The House Committee on Ways and Means

Kowabunga Dude!

Select a bill from the "Bill Text" section (you can use the "search" function to find a bill about a topic that interests you). Load the full text of the bill. Is this what you expected? Why or why not?

Teacher Plan

Welcome to the White House

Before the Internet exercise

1. Locate Washington, D.C., on a map of the United States. Compare its size and location with several states.
2. Lead a student discussion: Why do we have a White House? Brainstorm a list of reasons for having the White House and write the list on the board.
3. Ask students what they would expect to find if they visited the White House. Write their answers on the board.
4. Determine if any of your students have visited the White House. If so, ask those students to describe what they saw. They may even have souvenirs to share with the class.

After the Internet exercise

1. Ask the students what other information they would like to learn about the White House.
2. Post a United States highway map on the wall. Have students estimate the distance from their school to the White House.
3. Ask the students to brainstorm a new name for the White House. Compile the answers on the board.
4. E-mail the White House to ask a question about White House history.

Welcome to the White House

http://www.whitehouse.gov

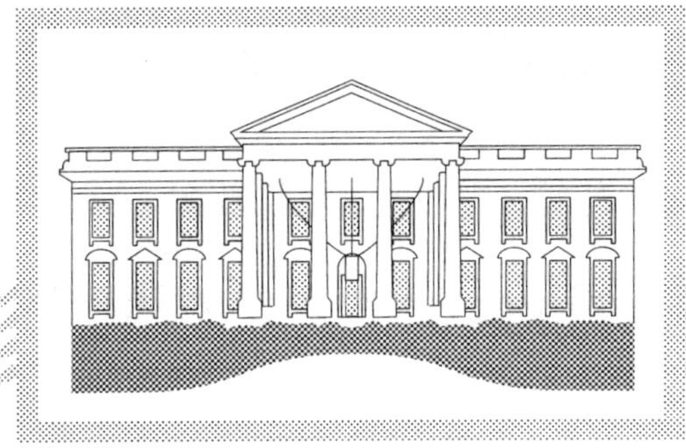

1. List the names of the following persons:
   - The President
   - The Vice-President
   - The First Lady
   - The spouse of the Vice-President
2. What is the mailing address of the White House?
3. What is the White House phone number?
4. What is the President's e-mail address?
5. Name two "Presidential Accomplishments" listed on the Web site.
6. Find the President's biography, and answer the following questions.
   - Where was the President born?
   - Where did the President attend college?
   - Who are the members of the President's immediate family?
7. Who is the Director of National Drug Policy?
8. What is "Today's Top Issue" as listed in the White House Briefing Room?
9. Go to the Social Statistics Briefing Room. Name four topics you find there.

Super Surfer

On your own paper, list the President's Cabinet departments. (Hint: There are more than a dozen.)

Kowabunga Dude!

Continue the "Super Surfer" activity by listing the Secretary (person in charge) of each Cabinet department. Follow the links to each department's Web site.

Teacher Plan

Benjamin Franklin: Glimpses of the Man

Before the Internet exercise

1. Lead a class discussion to determine what students know about Benjamin Franklin. About which areas of his life are they most knowledgeable?
2. Have students locate Philadelphia on a map and research Philadelphia in an encyclopedia. What landmarks are in Philadelphia? Have any of your students ever visited Philadelphia?
3. What was the world like in the late 1700s? Assign brief class reports on various aspects of life. Students should share their findings with the class.

After the Internet exercise

1. Create a bulletin board based on Benjamin Franklin's contributions to society. Each student should submit a graphic illustrating a contribution.
2. Lead a class exploration about cities, counties, and products bearing the name "Franklin." Are any of these names tributes to Benjamin Franklin?

Benjamin Franklin: Glimpses of the Man

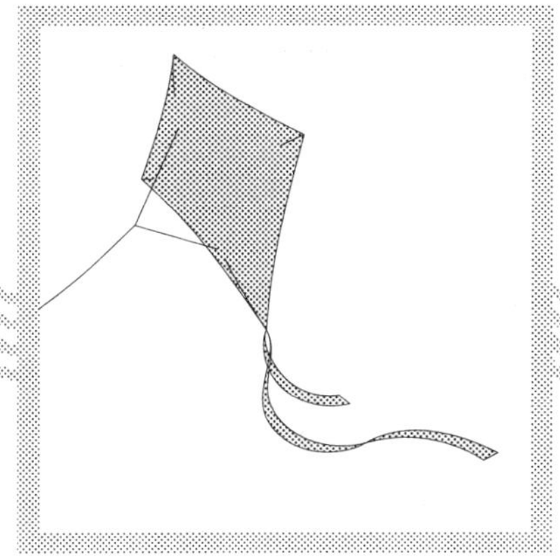

http://sln.fi.edu/franklin/rotten.html

1. You are invited to celebrate Benjamin Franklin's birthday. What date is his birthday?
2. Benjamin Franklin is known as a scientist. What "shocking discovery" did he make about lightning?
3. Franklin was also interested in weather. What was the name of the book in which he printed some of the first weather forecasts?
4. What interesting scientific event did Benjamin Franklin witness in Paris, France, in 1783?
5. Franklin is also known as a famous inventor. What improvement did he make to eyeglasses?
6. Although Benjamin Franklin did not "invent" electricity, what did he invent that helped protect buildings from lightning strikes?
7. How did Benjamin Franklin fight the American Revolution his own way?
8. Benjamin Franklin is the only person who signed all four of the documents that helped to create the United States of America. Name the four documents and the years in which they were signed.
9. Benjamin Franklin is not usually thought of as a musician, but he did invent a musical instrument. What was the name of the musical instrument that Franklin invented, and how was it played?
10. List five things that you would find at the Benjamin Franklin National Memorial.

Super Surfer

Visit the Franklin Institute Science Museum home page (it is linked to this site). Read about the current exhibits and write a few sentences describing one of them.

Kowabunga Dude!

In the "Printing" section, go to "What do you think Ben meant?" Make up a few of your own "words of wisdom" in the spirit and style of Benjamin Franklin's writing.

Teacher Plan

Biography.com

Before the Internet exercise

1. Lead a class discussion: What is the value of a biography? Why are people interested in biographies?
2. Lead a class discussion: What are the popular forms of biographies? What recent movies were biographies or featured biographical elements? How accurate are motion picture biographies?
3. Lead a class discussion: If you wrote a biography, whose life story would you write? Why does this person's life interest you?

After the Internet exercise

1. Assign a biography book report. Consult the media specialist about biographies that may have special interest for students.
2. Allow students to interview each other on videotape using the information from the Kowabunga Dude! section. A project plan called "Meet My Friend" can be found in *Video Projects for Elementary and Middle Schools* by Kyker and Curchy (Libraries Unlimited, 1995).
3. From your local library, media center, or video rental store, obtain a copy of a biography originally shown on the A&E Network, the sponsors of this page. (You may be able to record the program through the Cable in the Classroom program. Consult your media specialist for details.) Show segments of the biography to the class. Ask students to comment on the program.

Biography.com

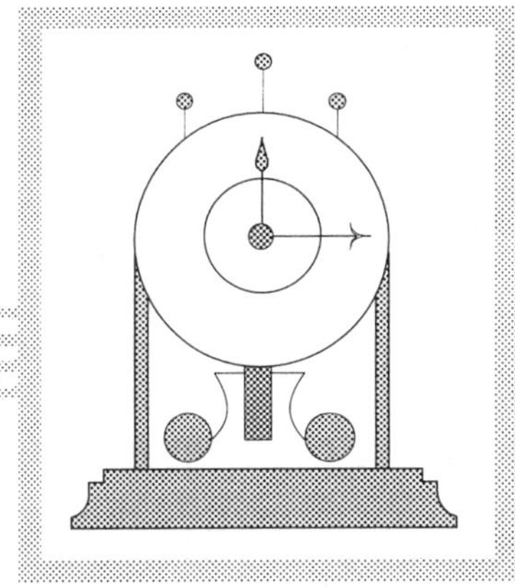

http://www.biography.com

Use the "Find" section to answer the following questions:

1. What city did Benjamin Banneker help create?
2. What was the name of Walt Disney's first full-length color cartoon film, and what year did it appear?
3. Eleanor Roosevelt was a member of two presidential families. Who were the presidents, and how was she related to them?
4. What major league baseball record does Hank Aaron still hold?
5. What happened when Amelia Earhart attempted to fly around the world in 1937?
6. By what nickname is William Cody better known? After his career in the Old West, how did Cody earn his living?
7. How many gold medals did Frederick "Carl" Lewis win in the 1984 Olympic Games? In which events did Lewis win gold medals?
8. For what special audience is Bob Hope well-known?
9. In which two law-making bodies did Barbara Jordan serve?
10. What other elected government office did Ronald Reagan hold before he was elected President?
11. For what album did B. B. King win a Grammy award?

Super Surfer

Go to the "Biography Play" section and take the biography quiz.

Kowabunga Dude!

Interview a classmate or a teacher and create a biography of that person similar to the entries found on this Web site.

Teacher Plan

Historic Timeline of Computing

Before the Internet exercise

1. Lead a class discussion: How do computers affect our lives?
2. Ask students about computer-related jobs. Make a list of every job that involves the use of a computer. How were these jobs performed before computers?
3. Obtain a copy of the classified advertisements "Help Wanted" section of your local newspaper. How many of the jobs require computer experience?

After the Internet exercise

1. Ask students to share the results of their Kowabunga Dude! activity with the class.
2. Create a timeline on the bulletin board. Ask each student to illustrate one of the computer milestones found on this Web site, and place their drawings on the correct points of the timeline.
3. Ask a local computer programmer or computer salesperson to speak to the class about recent and future computer technology developments.

Historic Timeline of Computing

http://www.tcm.org/history/timeline/index.html

1. In 1945 the phrase "computer bug" first appeared. What is the origin of this phrase?
2. In 1950, the first commercially produced computer was built. What was the name of the computer, who built it, and for whom was it built?
3. In 1961, the first industrial robot went into use. Which company used the robot and what was the robot's task?
4. The first popular video game was introduced in 1972. What was the name of this video game and which company manufactured it?
5. In 1974, the Xerox Alto featured a computer device that we now take for granted. What is the name of this device?
6. In 1976, the Apple I computer was introduced. Which two men started Apple Computers? What store agreed to sell their computers?
7. Three groundbreaking personal computers appeared in 1977. Name them.

Super Surfer

Using the "Resources" section of this Web site, find the "Careers in Computing" page. From the five career areas listed, select a career and write a paragraph describing it. Make sure to include projected earnings.

Kowabunga Dude!

Ask teachers and parents to describe their first experiences with computers. Make a list of the differences between those computers and the computer that you use. Present the list as a brief report to the class.

Teacher Plan

Kelley Blue Book: New Car Prices and Blue Book Values

Before the Internet exercise

1. Lead a class discussion: How important is the automobile in modern society? How would life be different without cars?
2. Consult an almanac or other source to determine the number of cars in the United States. Ask students to compare that figure with those for other countries.
3. Obtain an advertisement for used cars from a local newspaper. Write a description of several vehicles on the board. Ask students to estimate their values.

After the Internet exercise

1. Using the descriptions from question #3 above, check the value of the cars on the Web site. How close were the students?
2. Facilitate sharing of information gathered in the Kowabunga Dude! activity.
3. Ask a car salesperson to speak to the class about car pricing.

Kelley Blue Book: New Car Prices and Blue Book Values

http://www.kbb.com

This Web site is all about car prices. By entering the requested facts, you can find the value of almost any new or used car.

Use the "Goin' Shoppin" section of the "Used Car Values" page to find out how much you should expect to pay for the following used cars:

1. A 1991 VW Fox Sedan 2-door with a 4-speed transmission and 75,000 miles.
2. A 1995 Cadillac Fleetwood Sedan 4-door, with a V8 engine, automatic transmission, and 22,000 miles.
3. A 1983 Pontiac Firebird Trans Am Coupe 2-door with a V8, automatic transmission, and 45,000 miles.
4. A 1996 Honda Civic DX Sedan with 4 doors, a 4-cylinder engine, automatic transmission, and 11,000 miles.
5. A 1987 Subaru Brat GL Pickup truck with a 4-cylinder engine, a 4-speed transmission, and 100,000 miles in good condition.
6. A 1995 Chevrolet Cavalier Sedan with 4 doors, automatic transmission, and 40,000 miles.

Super Surfer

Use the "Important Sites" selection to find Microsoft Carpoint (or simply type the URL **http://carpoint.msn.com/loancalc**). Determine the monthly payment on a new vehicle of your choice (use the "New Car Pricing" section to find base prices). You may have to call a bank or check the newspaper to find the current interest rate.

Kowabunga Dude!

Ask a parent, grandparent, or teacher about their first car purchase. Ask them to describe their cars and how much they paid for them. Find out how their cars were different from cars currently on the market and how they were the same. Present your findings to the class.

Teacher Plan

Learn2.com—The Ability Utility

Before the Internet exercise

1. List tasks that students have learned. Ask them when, where, and why they learned these tasks. Ask them who taught the task to them.
2. Demonstrate a simple activity (polishing shoes, tying a necktie, etc.). Ask students to list the steps in order. You may have to repeat the activity several times.
3. Assign a writing exercise. Students should select a simple task with which they are familiar and then write a paragraph describing the step-by-step process of doing this task. A reader should be able to perform the task after reading the instructions in the paragraph.

After the Internet exercise

1. Lead a class discussion: Other than this Web site, in what ways do we learn to do things?
2. Ask students to list tasks that they would like to see on this Web site.
3. Assign a brief demonstration speech based on the material from this Web site or the paragraphs written earlier.

Learn2.com—The Ability Utility

http://www.Learn2.com

This Web site is all about learning to do things, like tying a knot, changing a tire, or shining your shoes. Some of the skills are more exciting, and they're all pretty important.

Take a few minutes to explore this Web site on your own. Notice that the tasks are arranged in categories for easy browsing.

1. List five of those categories.
2. Choose a category that interests you. Write down that category.
3. Select a learning activity from the list and write it down.
4. List the steps needed to complete this activity.
5. How much time is required to learn this task?
6. List the materials that you will need to perform this activity.

Your assignment is to learn the activity described in the lesson you have chosen. You may need help from an adult. If the lesson you have selected is too difficult or impractical, you may have to select another.

Prepare a brief class presentation about the skill that you learned.

Super Surfer

Access the Top Ten list of requested learning activities. Write that list in order. How many of those things do you already know how to do?

Kowabunga Dude!

With parent or teacher permission, use the "Talk 2 Us" feature of the Web site to send an e-mail to the authors of Learn2.com. You can even request an activity that you would like to see a lesson about.

Answer Key

Many of the questions in this book are open-ended or site-specific (e.g., What is the forecast for your region this week?). Those questions are omitted from the answer key; only questions for which all students will have the same answer are included. In some cases, entire activity sheets are omitted from this answer key because all questions are open-ended or site-specific. No answers are provided for the Super Surfer and Kowabunga Dude! sections.

Bartlett, John. 1901. Familiar Quotations

2. "I have gathered a posie of other men's flowers, and nothing but the thread that binds them is mine own."
3. 1875

The Complete Works of William Shakespeare

1. Full fathom five... *The Tempest*
   He that hath a beard... *Much Ado About Nothing*
   The devil can cite... *The Merchant of Venice*
   What's in a name?... *Romeo and Juliet*
   A horse! A horse!... *King Richard III*
   Cowards die many times... *Julius Caesar*
   We cannot all be masters... *Othello*
2. Comedy, history, and tragedy. The arrangement of the plays into the three categories began with the First Folio, which was printed in 1623, seven years after Shakespeare's death.
3. Poetry
4. *Two Gentlemen of Verona*, which was probably written around 1598.
5. The last play written was *Henry VIII*, in 1613. A cannon firing is part of the play. During one of the first performances of this play the cannon started the fire that burned the Globe Theatre to the ground.

The Page at Pooh Corner

1. The books were written by A. A. Milne and illustrated by E. H. Shepard.

2. The books were first published in the 1920s.
3. Edward Bear
4. Thirty-three languages.
5. Alan Alexander Milne was born January 18, 1882.
6. Christopher Robin Milne. He received a teddy bear, which would become the inspiration for Winnie-the-Pooh.
7. Cotchford farm, near London.
8. Winnie-the Pooh, Eeyore, Piglet, Kanga, Roo and Tigger are based on stuffed animals. The stuffed animals are displayed in the Central Children's Room of the Donnell Library Center, a branch of the New York Public Library.
9. The real Winnie was an American black bear, originally owned by an army officer named Harry Colebourn.
10. Kenny Loggins.

National Earthquake Information Center

1. The National Earthquake Information Center is located at 1711 Illinois Street in Golden, Colorado (on the Colorado School of Mines Campus).
5. Alaska and California have the most earthquakes. Florida and North Dakota have the fewest earthquakes.
6. An earthquake can last two or three minutes.
7. Eighteen major earthquakes and one great earthquake. Forty-nine thousand minor earthquakes.
8. The most destructive earthquake ever recorded was on January 23, 1556, in China (Shansi). 830,000 people were killed.
9. The largest earthquake in the United States occurred in Prince William Sound, Alaska, on March 28, 1964.

Volcano World

From the "Ask a Volcanologist" questions:

1. Lava and magma both describe molten rock. Magma is molten rock below the surface, and lava is molten rock that has erupted from a volcano.
2. Lava is very hot. The temperature range is from 700°C to 1250°C.

3. There is usually a lot of rain, thunder, and lightning during a volcanic eruption. Thick fog is also often present.

The Heart

1. In an average lifetime, the heart beats more than two and a half billion times.
2. Infant — 120 beats per minute

   7-year old — 90 beats per minute

   18-year old — 70 beats per minute
3. Four cavities — 2 atria and 2 ventricles
4. Aorta
5. Pulmonary artery
6. Five liters
7. A, B, AB, and O. Type O is considered the "universal donor."
8. Stethoscope
9. A murmur indicates that blood is seeping through the closed valve separating the atrium and ventricle.
10. Less exercise and a high fat diet
11. Christiaan Barnard in 1967
12. Willem DeVries, an American surgeon, implanted the first permanent artificial heart. It was designed by Robert Jarvik, an American physician.

The Faces of Science

1. Specialized in kidney surgery and research
2. . . . to conduct and publish research in her field.
3. Chemurgy
5. Space science (space navigation)
6. Answers may vary. The Web site highlights the following:
   the heating plant and power station for the University of Iowa
   a sewage treatment plant in Grand Rapids, Michigan
   an airfield in Tuskegee, Alabama
   Tidal Basin bridge and seawall in Washington, D.C.
   Whitehurst Freeway in Washington, D.C.

8. Energy
9. The Tuskegee Airmen
10. The blood bank
11. Dr. Williams performed the first open heart surgery.
12. Insects; specifically ants and spiders

International Space Station

All answers are subject to rescheduling.

1. Zarya, a Functional Cargo Block—FGB
2. Russia and the United States of America
3. January 2004
4. Life sciences, Earth sciences, space science, microgravity science, and engineering research
5. 16 nations (this may change)
6. European Space Agency

From the "Frequently Asked Questions" Section

1. 44 launches
2. July 1999
3. Average of 220 miles

NASA Astronaut Biographies

1. Lieutenant Colonel. He was a fighter pilot and a test pilot.
2. Four missions (as of August, 1998)
3. He was a helicopter and jet pilot in the United States Navy.
4. Solar physics and astrophysics
5. January 1999 (dated text)
6. June 1991
7. Pilot. Hammond is currently the Branch Chief of the Astronaut Office Safety Branch, where he monitors all T-38, shuttle, and space station safety issues.
8. STS-68 (September 30 to October 11, 1994) and STS-81 (January 12–22, 1997)
9. Punjab Engineering College, India; University of Texas; University of Colorado

From the "Additional Astronaut Information" page

1. Humans must wear spacesuits while working in space because (1) there is no atmospheric pressure in space, and (2) there is no oxygen in space.

The Nine Planets

1. 5800 degrees K
2. Hydrogen and helium
3. The sun is about 4.5 billion years old. It will continue for about 5 billion more years.
4. Heavily cratered
5. Mariner 2 in 1962
6. Mars Pathfinder
7. Phobos and Deimos
8. Jupiter is 90% hydrogen and 10% helium. It does not have a solid surface.
9. The Great Red Spot is an oval about 12,000 by 25,000 km, big enough to hold two Earths.
10. The ring particles seem to be composed primarily of water ice, but they may also include rocky particles with icy coatings.
11. 18; Titan is the largest.
12. William Herschel
13. Uranus's atmosphere is about 83% hydrogen, 15% helium and 2% methane.
14. Neptune's most prominent feature was the Great Dark Spot. It disappeared from view. It may have totally dissipated, or it may be masked in the atmosphere.
15. Pluto is very small and very far away. A spacecraft has not been sent there. Pluto's satellite is Charon.

World Wildlife Fund

1. 116 countries (as of August, 1998)
3. Donations from individuals
5. Species are on the list because "despite national and international protection, (they) are particularly threatened by illegal and unsustainable trade."

Caribbean Conservation Corporation/Sea Turtle Survival League

1. The CCC was founded in 1959 by Mr. Joshua B. Powers.
2. Gainesville, Florida
3. Satellite telemetry
4. Green turtles
5. Tracking studies are based on nesting, and only the females build nests.
6. Between Melbourne and Wabasso, along Florida's east coast; 20.5 miles of beach
7. (1) Quiet sandy beach (2) with little or no artificial light
8. Loggerhead turtles, green turtles, and mammoth leatherback turtles
9. Dr. Carr was born in 1909 in Mobile, Alabama. He taught at the University of Florida.
10. Loggerhead turtle, green turtle, black turtle, leatherback turtle, hawksbill turtle
11. Kingdom: Animalia
    Phylum: Chordata
    Class: Reptilia
    Order: Testudines
    Suborder: Cryptodira
    Family: Dermochelyidae
    Genus: Caretta
    Species: caretta
12. 80–120 eggs
13. 1 in 1,000

Sea World and Busch Gardens Animal Resources Page

1. Order: Cetacea
   Family: Monodontidae
   Genus: Delphinapterus
   Species: leucas
2. "They are known to prey on about 100 different kinds of primarily bottom-dwelling animals. They eat octopus; squid; crabs; shrimp; clams; snails; sandworms; and fishes such as capelin, cod, herring, smelt, and flounder."

"Belugas eat approximately 2.5% to 3% of their body weight per day, about 18.2 to 27.2 kg (40-60 lb.)"

3. "Bottlenose dolphins inhabit temperate and tropical waters throughout the world," including the Pacific Ocean, Atlantic Ocean, Indian Ocean, and Mediterranean Sea.
4. Hearing and eyesight
5. 20 years or less, although some have lived as long as 48 years
6. White, red, orange, yellow, green, blue, and purple
7. Defense; moving food to the mouth
8. Several answers are provided on Web site.
9. Females average 1.4 m (4.6 ft.) and 90 kg (198 lb.). Males average 1.7 m (5.6 ft.) and 180 kg (397 lb.).
10. "The gorilla's pot-bellied appearance comes from an enlarged intestine needed to accommodate and digest the bulky food items on which this great ape feeds."
11. A noisy charge, chest-beating, hooting, running, tearing plants, slapping the ground.
12. There are 17 species of penguins. Students will name various species.
13. "Penguin species are found on every continent in the Southern Hemisphere. They are abundant on many temperate and subantarctic islands. Different species thrive in varying climates, ranging from Galcipagos penguins on tropical islands at the equator to emperor penguins restricted to the pack ice of Antarctica."
14. Several answers are listed on the Web site.

Worm World

1. Earthworm, leech, planaria, tapeworm, bearded worm
2. Worms are slimy because they're covered with mucus. The mucus keeps them moist, so they can breathe through their skin.
3. 120 million years
4. 1 million (or more)
5. Castings are worm excrement. The castings contain recycled nutrients from the debris the worms eat.

6. South American earthworms can grow to be 8 feet long and ¾ of an inch in diameter; they can weigh more than 1 pound.
7. Flatworm
8. Planaria live in ponds and streams.

Worms as Recyclers

1. Answers will include: mold, bacteria, mites, beetles, centipedes, and earthworms.
2. They break things down into valuable nutrients that can be used by other plants and animals.

Body Parts

1. A worm eats decaying leaves by pushing its pharynx (throat) out of its mouth to grab leaves and pull them back into its mouth. After it coats the leaves with saliva, it pushes them down its esophagus to a storage compartment, called the crop, and then on to the gizzard. The gizzard contains stones the worm has swallowed. When the food reaches the gizzard, the worm uses its strong muscles to make the stones grind and crush the leaves. After the leaves are ground up, they pass on to the intestine, where digestive juices break down the food even more. Then some of the food passes into the bloodstream.
2. Small stones that the worm has swallowed, combined with strong stomach muscles.

The Wolf Sanctuary

1. Washington University's Tyson Research Center
2. The Wolf Sanctuary was founded in 1971 by noted naturalist Dr. Marlin Perkins, his wife Carol, and a group of individuals concerned about the plight of canids.
3. The Wolf Sanctuary (1) helps inform and educate people about the plight of wolves, and (2) promotes the protection of the remaining wild wolves and their habitat.
4. Red wolf, Mexican gray wolf, maned wolf, and Iranian gray wolf
5. 50 acres
6. "Each wolf gets 2 pounds per day of dry dog food; either Purina Hi-Pro or Pro-Plan Lite, both from Ralston Purina or Mazuri

Exotic Canine diet, from Purina Mills, Inc. The wolves also hunt any small animals that stray into their enclosures, such as raccoon and opossum. The dry food is supplemented by large cow bones from Zerna Meats in Labadie, Missouri."

7. No. The wolves are wild animals. The wolves are kept wild so that they can survive if they are released into their natural habitat.
8. The wolves have lost too much habitat because of the encroachment of civilization.

From the "Wolf Factoids" section (under "Facts and Information")

1. 42 teeth
2. Wolves howl to assemble the pack, identify individuals, and express their emotional state.
3. Gray wolf and red wolf

The Tiger Information Center

1. Bengal tigers, Indochinese tigers, Siberian tigers, Sumatran tigers, South China tigers
2. Asia
3. 5,000–7,400 tigers (1998)
4. Bali tiger, Caspian tiger, and Javan tiger
5. About 437–506 Siberian tigers still exist in the wild. About 490 captive Siberian tigers are in zoos.
6. The Siberian tiger weighs the most. The Sumatran tiger is the smallest.
7. The night vision of tigers is six times better than that of humans.
8. Tigers scratch on trees to mark their territory.
9. The life span of tigers in the wild is thought to be about 10–15 years.
10. Wild tigers can eat 40 pounds of meat at one time.
11. Habitat loss, poaching, and trade in tiger parts

From the "Common Misconceptions about Tigers" section:

1. Yes. Unlike most cat species, tigers like water and are good swimmers. In tropical climates, tigers frequently spend time lying in water to cool off.

The Cat Fanciers' Association

1. The Cat Fanciers' Association is the world's largest registry of pedigreed cats.
3. "While cats instinctively fall feet first and may survive falls from high places, they also may receive broken bones in the process."

   "Most cats like milk, but do not need it if properly nourished. Also, many will get diarrhea if they drink too much milk. If it is given at all, the amount should be small and infrequent."

   "Actually, most warm-blooded mammals, including cats, bats, skunks and ferrets, can carry rabies. Like dogs, cats should be vaccinated regularly according to local laws."

   "Cats use their whiskers as "feelers" but not to maintain their balance."

   "Such licking actually can slow the healing process and further damage the wound."
4. Uniqueness, pleasing appearance, unusual markings, and sweet disposition
5. There are 33 pedigreed breeds for showing in the Championship Class, 2 breeds in the Provisional Class, and 2 breeds in the Miscellaneous Class (as of August 1998).

FitLife

1. illness
2. keep us healthy and fit.
4. (1) Bread, cereals, rice and pasta, (2) Vegetable group, (3) Fruit group
5. No. (Examples will vary.)
6. You need 6-8 glasses per day; you will need more to replace body fluids lost when you sweat.
7. Water will help fill your stomach and make you feel full, so you will want to eat less.
8. Skipping meals is not a good idea. It causes you to lose control and overeat.
9. Stress is not always bad. Stress allows us to become involved in what we're doing and have a zest for life.
10. Check with your physician (doctor).

11. Frequency, Intensity, and Time (or Duration). The three phases of training are: warm up, training period, cool down.

The American Lung Association: "Learn About Lung Health"

1. 14.6 million Americans (in 1998)
2. Several answers are listed on the Web site
3. Asthma is an ongoing disease. You live with it every day.
4. (1) Coughing during or after exercise, (2) shortness of breath, (3) wheezing sound when breathing, (4) tightness in chest
5. 4.8 million children
6. 430,700 lives each year (1998)
7. $97.2 billion each year
9. Several answers are listed on the Web site.
10. Nicotine
11. Taste of cigarettes, smell of cigarettes, feel of cigarettes, (4) linked to other activities
12. Heart disease, cancer and emphysema

Fruit and Vegetable Nutrition Center

1. dietary fiber
2. 110 calories
3. 0
4. 5 grams
5. 25
6. 20%
7. Cantaloupe, carrot, sweet potato
8. Several answers are listed on the Web site.

Fast Food Facts — Interactive Food Finder

1. The Minnesota Attorney General's Office

On Broadway — WWW Information Page

3. Antoinette Perry
4. 1947; Arthur Miller won Outstanding Playwright

The History of Superhero Comic Books

1. The Yellow Kid
2. *Funnies on Parade*; The comic books were not sold. They were given away with coupons for Proctor & Gamble products.
3. *New Fun Comics* included comics that were not printed in the newspaper.
4. *Action Comics* #1
5. Batman
6. Prince Namor the Sub-Mariner
7. Robin, the Boy Wonder. He assisted Batman.
8. The Justice Society of America. They appeared in *All Star Comics* #3.
9. The Nazis
10. Archie Andrews

Carnegie Hall

1. 1891
2. Leopold Damrosch; Walter Damrosch
3. Andrew Carnegie, a steel tycoon
4. William Burnet Tuthill; The corner of 57th Street and 7th Avenue in New York City.
5. Peter Ilyich Tchaikovsky
6. Damrosch organized concerts specifically for children.
7. "The rock performer Sting presents his fifth benefit at Carnegie Hall to aid the rain forests on April 12, 1995. Assisting artists for this event were Jon Bon Jovi, Billy Joel, Elton John, Jessye Norman, Paul Simon, Bruce Springsteen, and James Taylor." (Students may name any three of the assisting artists.)

Medieval and Renaissance Instruments

1. Herdsmen (shepherds)
2. "The name of the Crumhorn comes from the German *krumhorn* (also *krummhorn, krumphorn*), meaning curved horn (or the older English *crump*, meaning curve)."

3. The dulcimer is played by striking the strings with small hammers.
4. The horn of a chamois or ox.
5. In the Middle Ages the strings for musical instruments were made from twisted animal gut (usually from sheep). Horse hair and even silk were used as well.
6. "Before 1300 the instrument was often long enough to require two performers, one to crank, and one to push the keys."
7. A flattened letter *s*
8. Pine, sycamore, cedar, yew, cypress
9. By pumping a bellows made of sheepskin and wood with the left hand while, at the same time, playing a button-type keyboard with the right hand.
10. A trombone; "push-pull"
11. The tuba
12. The Hebrew culture; ibex, ram.

The National Park Service ParkNet

1. Hodgenville, Kentucky
2. The park gets about 1.3 million visitors per year; the park is least crowded from mid-November through March.
3. Answers may include: Ford's Theater National Historic Site, Arlington House, The White House, the Old Post Office, the Frederick Douglas House, Rock Creek Park, Manassas National Battlefield Park, Prince William Forest Park, and the George Washington Memorial Parkway.
4. The Carver Museum, The Oaks (Home of Booker T. Washington), The Chappie James Museum
5. Rainbow Bridge is the world's largest natural bridge.
6. More than 15,000. A petroglyph is an image carved in rock by prehistoric and historic Native American and Hispanic people.
7. George Washington, Thomas Jefferson, Theodore Roosevelt, and Abraham Lincoln
8. Both the Declaration of Independence and the U.S. Constitution were created there.
9. The Earth's most massive volcano is Mauna Loa. The world's most active volcano is Kilauea.

The United States Show Caves Directory

1. Mammoth Cave in Kentucky
2. Mariana, Florida
3. Most Florida caves are filled with water. The cave system at Florida Caverns is not.
5. The Big Room measures almost 360,000 square feet.
6. Kings River Canyon is 8,000 feet deep and was created over a 300,000-year period.
7. The Dripstone Trail is wheelchair-accessible (with a strong assistant).
8. The cave is lined with a 6-inch layer of calcite, which gives the cave a jeweled appearance.
9. The wind in the cave develops as this vast cave system strives to equilibrate with shifting atmospheric pressures above ground. The cave thus serves as a natural barometer, with inhalent (incoming) breezes signifying clear and calm high pressure weather systems and exhalent (outgoing) breezes indicating stormy low pressure conditions.

The Official Site of the Negro Baseball Leagues

1. The Negro Baseball Leagues were founded in 1920 to provide opportunities for minorities to play professional baseball. At that time, minorities were not allowed to play major league baseball.

From the "History" section:

1. Answers will include Willie Mays, Ernie Banks, Jackie Robinson, Hank Aaron, Roy Campanella, Monte Irvin.
2. The Negro Baseball Leagues Museum is in Kansas City, Missouri. It opened in January, 1991. The Kansas City Monarchs.

From the "Teams" section:

1. The Grays won nine straight league pennants.
2. Willie Mays

From the "Players" section:

1. In 1934, Buck Leonard was paid $125 a month plus 60 cents a day for meals.
2. The Brooklyn Dodgers; Robinson was the first African American player to sign with a major league baseball team.

The All-American Girls Professional Baseball League

1. 1943 to 1954
2. The league was invented by Philip K. Wrigley. He owned the Chicago Cubs.
3. The main factor was a drop in attendance. The main reasons for decreasing attendance and a resulting decrease in revenues included the return of teams to local control, instead of league control, in 1951; the decline of the local fan base, due in part to the rise of other forms of recreation and entertainment; the advent of major league games being televised in the early 1950s; and the lack of "rookie teams" as a way to recruit new baseball talent.

   Another page on this Web site states "The league was dissolved as the result of the men returning home from the war and the advent of television."
4. More than 600
5. The Kenosha Comets, the Racine Belles, the Rockford Peaches, and the South Bend Blue Sox
6. In 1948 10 teams competed.
7. Joanne Weaver batted .429 in 1954.
8. The Racine Belles; the Kalamazoo Lassies
9. La Vonne "Pepper" Paire-Davis and Nalda "Bird" Phillips
10. Sophie Kurys, also known as the Flint Flash, played in the league from 1943–1952 and stole 1,114 bases.

A Guide to the Great Sioux Nation

1. South Dakota
2. The dialects were Dakota, Nakota, and Lakota.
3. North Dakota, South Dakota, Nebraska, Wyoming, and Montana
4. The trail crosses over the traditional hunting grounds of the Teton.
5. Gold
6. General George Custer
7. The Lakota call them "he sapa" or "black mountains."
8. "A striking landscape of buttes and spires (that) rises abruptly out of the South Dakota prairie. When they first encountered these unusual formations, the Lakota aptly called them 'mako sica,' meaning 'bad land.' "

9. Crazy Horse, a legendary Lakota leader. When completed, it will stand 563 feet high and 641 feet long.
10. The porcupine
11. "Wacipi"
12. Indian taco, Indian fry bread, and "wojapi," a fruit pudding
13. (1) At the "Grand Entry" to pay respect to the dancers and (2) for the Great Sioux Nation's national anthem

Kanazawa City

1. Hokuriku
2. 1583
3. The Maeda family
4. 450,000
5. The Japan Alps
6. Hakusan National Park and Noto Peninsula National Park
7. The Sai and the Asano rivers
8. August is the hottest month. The average temperature is 28.9°C (84.0°F).
9. (1) Kado, the way of flowers, (2) Sado, the way of tea, (3) Shodo, the way of writing, (4) Judo, the way of flexibility, (5) Kendo, the way of the sword, and (6) Kyudo, the way of the bow
10. Kaga Yuzen—dyeing silk material; Noh—dramatic performance; Kanazawa Shikki—lacquerware decorated with gold dust; Kanazawa Haku —gold leaf work; Ohiyaki—pottery.
11. (1) Buffalo, New York; (2) Irkutsk, Irkutsu; (3) Porto Alegre, Brazil; (4) Ghent, Belgium; (5) Nancy, France; and (6) Suzhou, China

United Nations Home Page

1. The United Nations officially came into existence on October 24, 1945.
3. Trygve Lie of Norway
4. 185 (as of August 1998; subject to change)
5. France, Russian Federation, United Kingdom, United States, China

6. The Hague
7. New York City
8. From the glossary: "peace-keeping operation; PKO [noncombat military operations undertaken by outside forces with the consent of all major belligerent parties and designed to monitor and facilitate the implementation of an existing truce agreement in support of diplomatic efforts to reach a political settlement"
10. The 15 Member States of the Security Council are in charge of peacekeeping operations.
11. Division for Ocean Affairs and the Law of the Sea
12. UNEP—United Nations Environment Programme
    UNDRO—United Nations Disaster Relief Organization
    UNICEF—United Nations Children's Fund
    WFP—World Food Programme
    WHO—World Health Organization

THOMAS–U.S. Congress on the Internet

1. Thomas Jefferson

Welcome to the White House

1. Subject to change every four years
2. 1600 Pennsylvania Avenue, Washington, D.C. 20500
3. (202) 456-1414
4. president@whitehouse.gov
6. Subject to change every four years
7. Subject to change

Benjamin Franklin: Glimpses of the Man

1. January 17, 1706
2. Franklin discovered that lightning was an electrical current.
3. *Poor Richard's Almanack*
4. The world's first known hot air balloon flight
5. He had two pairs of spectacles cut in half and put half of each lens in a single frame. Today, we call them bifocals.
6. The lightning rod

7. "Ben used his diplomacy skills to serve his fellow countrymen. His role in the American Revolution was not played out on the battlefields like George Washington, but rather in the halls and staterooms of governments. His clear vision of the way things should be, and his skill in both writing and negotiating, helped him to shape the future of the United States of America."
8. Declaration of Independence (1776); the Treaty of Alliance, Amity, and Commerce with France (1778); the Treaty of Peace among England, France, and the United States (1782); and (4) the Constitution (1787)
9. The glass armonica. This simple musical instrument was played by touching the edge of the spinning glass with damp fingers.

Biography.com

1. District of Columbia (Washington, D.C.)
2. Snow White and the Seven Dwarfs (1937)
3. She was a niece of Theodore Roosevelt and the wife (and distant cousin) of Franklin Roosevelt.
4. He holds many baseball records, including most lifetime runs batted in (2,297) and most years with 30 or more home runs (15). But the most famous record is most career home runs (755).
5. "She ceased communications on July 2, shortly after leaving New Guinea with her navigator Frederick Noonan. Several extensive searches revealed nothing.
6. Buffalo Bill. "He decided to capitalize on his fame by organizing "Buffalo Bill's Wild West Show.... With himself as the star and with other talented marksmen and riders—including Annie Oakley — and featuring a mock battle with Indians, the show toured before appreciative audiences throughout America and Europe for 30 years."
7. Four; 100 m, 200 m, 4×100 m relay, and long jump
8. Military troops in the field
9. The Texas Senate and U.S. House of Representatives
10. Governor of California
11. *There Must Be a Better World Somewhere*

Historic Timeline of Computing

1. On September 9, 1945, Grace Hopper recorded the first actual computer "bug" — a moth stuck between the relays on the Harvard Mark II computer. The first computer "bug" was really a bug!
2. ERA 1101, built by Engineering Research Associates of Minneapolis for the U.S. Navy
3. Dwight D. Eisenhower and Adlai Stevenson; the computer correctly predicted a victory for Eisenhower, even though opinion polls forcasted a big win for Stevenson.
4. TRADIC was built by AT&T Bell Laboratories.
5. Pong, manufactured by Atari video games
6. A mouse
7. Steve Wosniak and Steve Jobs; Byte Shop
8. The Commodore PET, the Apple II, and the Tandy Radio Shack TRS-80

Index

Index to Web Sites

TechKNOWLEDGE!

Resources from ***Teacher Ideas Press***

THE INTERNET RESOURCE DIRECTORY FOR K–12 TEACHERS AND LIBRARIANS, 98/99 Edition
Elizabeth B. Miller

This award-winning annual offers you access to current, accurate, useful information about the network. Designed for educators, it organizes material by curriculum areas. Sites are annotated and screened, and this edition has increased emphasis on sites with lesson plans. FREE URL ADDRESS UPDATES listed at www.lu.com. **All levels.**
Fall 1998 ca.325p. 7x10 paper ISBN 1-56308-718-9

THE INTERNET AND INSTRUCTION
Activities and Ideas
2d Edition
Ann E. Barron and Karen S. Ivers

Technology in the classroom? It's easy! Designed for educators and students, this guide to telecommunications and the Internet demystifies the technology and provides relevant, feasible, and easy-to-implement ideas and activities. Expanded coverage of Web resources and cross-curricular activities are available in this new edition. **Grades 4–12.**
xi, 244p. 8½x11 paper ISBN 1-56308-613-1

DIG THAT SITE!
Exploring Archaeology, History, and Civilization on the Internet
Gary M. Garfield and Suzanne M. McDonough

Explore the lost culture of Pompeii, Mayan ruins in Honduras, temples in the Middle East, and many more historical sites around the globe—using the Internet! Organized by continent, this book has units that let learners research other cultures and civilizations by "visiting" actual people and places from the past. **Grades 3–8.**
ix, 135p. 8½x11 paper ISBN 1-56308-534-8

VIRTUAL FIELD TRIPS
Gail Cooper and Gary Cooper

From the bottom of the ocean floor to outer space, these fascinating Internet field trips allow you to take students almost anywhere! Organized by subject and cross-referenced for quick and easy access, this book leads you and your students to the most exciting, educational, and innovative Web sites on the Internet. **Grades K–12.**
xvii, 168p. 7x10 paper ISBN 1-56308-557-7

THE INTERNET FOR NEWBIES
An Easy Access Guide
Constance D. Williams

Are you a *newbie* on the Internet? Don't go surfing without this book! You will learn what's out there, how to find it, and what to do with it when you get it. Written for beginning users, this book will save you hours of time and help you avoid frustrating pitfalls. **Grades K–12.**
xv, 129p. 8½x11 paper ISBN 1-56308-483-X

For a FREE catalog or to place an order, please contact:

Teacher Ideas Press
Dept. B77 · P.O. Box 6633 · Englewood, CO 80155-6633
1-800-237-6124, ext. 1 · Fax: 303-220-8843 · E-mail: lu-books@lu.com

Check out the TIP Web site!
www.lu.com/tip